FIERY REBIRTH
A PHOENIX'S TALE

Copyright © 2024 by Ash A. Zander.

ISBN 978-1-963917-09-3 (softcover)
ISBN 978-1-963917-10-9 (hardback))
ISBN 978-1-963917-11-6 (ebook)

All rights reserved. No part of this book may be reproduced or transmitted in any form or by any means, electronic or mechanical, including photocopying, recording, or by any information storage and retrieval system without express written permission from the author, except in the case of brief quotations embodied in critical reviews and certain other noncommercial uses permitted by copyright law.

Printed in the United States of America.

Table of Contents

Morning Prayer of Gratitude	1
The Strength in Silence	5
Gift of Life	7
Everlasting Love: A Tribute to Motherhood	9
Silent Tears	11
Echoes of Hop	13
Walking the Path of Loss	15
Golden Mother, Endless Light	17
In Life's Guiding Embrace	19
Serenade of Love	21
Hope Amidst Chaos	23
Mother hurried treasure	25
Guiding Light	27
Embracing Life's Canvas	29
The Beauty of life	31
An Ode to an Unknown Hero	33
Love's Radiance: A Valentine's Day Celebration	35
Harmony of Hearts	37
A Haven Within	39
A Heart's Surrender	41
Harmony Within	43
Echoes of Serenity	45
Blessed in Affection	47
Whispers of Affection	49
The Tapestry of Time	52

Life's Priceless Treasure	54
Sent from Above	56
True Friendship's Glow	58
Wings of Self-Belief	60
Mother's Love, a Sacred Vine	62
Dignity's Light	64
Whispers in the Dark	66
Learning to Be Loved	67
A Mother's Legacy	69
Dreams With Mama	71
Eternal Embrace	73
Mamma's Belief	75
Fathers Guiding Light	77
Eulogy: "The Light We've Lost"	78
Wealth Unveiled	79
Eulogy: "A Soul's Journey Unveiled"	80
Mother's Embrace	81
Eternal Love	84
In Every Life, I Choose You, Mother	86
A Perfect Mother	88
Mother's Courageous Soul	90
A Mother's Treasure	92
Mother's Grace	95
Dance of Love	98
The Wisdom of Understanding	100
Mother's Radiance	102
Building Bridges	104
Regrets of Time Well Spent	105

Unspoken Strength	107
A Brother Heartbeat	109
Bonds Beyond Blood	112
Love Intrinsic Thread	114
Treasured Moments with My Boy	116
Harmony Restored: A Journey of Love and Acceptance	119
Dreams of Us- from 32992	122
A Prayer for the End of the Workday	124

Poem

Morning Prayer of Gratitude

In the quiet of the morning's glow,
My gratitude to you, dear God, I show.
For the love that warms my soul each day,
And the grace that guides me on my way.

Your strength, my steadfast friend in need,
Through every trial, you plant the seed.
As I face the dawn with uncertain eyes,
I find comfort in your watchful skies.

With humility, I seek your light,
To lead me through both day and night.
In life's vast tapestry, I pray to see,
The wisdom to choose what's best for me.

With each step, I feel your grace,
Guiding me to a better place.
May your hand hold mine throughout the day,
And may my choices reflect your way.

In Jesus' name, I offer this plea,
Grateful for your love that sets me free.
For with you, dear God, all is possible,
In your embrace, I find my soul's solace. Amen.

Description:

In the serene quiet of the morning, I pause to express my gratitude, dear God, for the warmth of your love and the gentle embrace of your grace. Your presence fills me with a sense of peace and reassurance as I prepare to face the challenges of the day ahead.

Throughout my journey, your strength has been my constant companion, guiding me through the twists and turns of life's path. Your unwavering support helps me navigate the uncertainties that greet me each day, instilling in me the courage to persevere and overcome obstacles.

As I stand on the threshold of a new day, I am mindful of the uncertainties that lie ahead. Yet, in the knowledge that your watchful eyes are upon me, I find solace and comfort. Your presence is my beacon of hope, illuminating the way forward and giving me the strength to face whatever may come.

With humility, I submit to your guidance, trusting that your divine will shall light my path and lead me in the right direction. In the vast tapestry of life's choices, I seek your wisdom to make decisions that align with your purpose and bring me closer to fulfilling my destiny.

With each step I take, I strive to walk in the light of your grace, acknowledging your presence in every aspect of my journey. May your guiding hand continue to lead me through the day and may the choices I make reflect the goodness and love that you instil within me.

In the name of Jesus, I offer this prayer, grateful for the assurance that, with you, all things are possible. Amen.

Poem

Unspoken Strength

How did you do it, dear mother mine,
Enduring ridicule, yet with grace you shine?
Day in and out, your own children's jest,
Yet in the eyes of the world, you're truly blessed.

Your secret strength, you held it tight,
Beneath your smile, hid a silent fight.
Valued and loved by the community's gaze,
Your inner turmoil concealed in a silent maze.

What was your secret, mother dear?
That shielded you from every tear.
You took it with you to the grave's silent rest,
Leaving your children to ponder, to jest.

Your unspoken strength, a beacon bright,
Guiding us through the darkest night.
Though your secret remains a mystery untold,
Your legacy of resilience and love, forever bold.

Description:

This poem delves into the profound strength and resilience exhibited by a mother who faces ridicule from her own children while still being cherished and respected by the wider community. The speaker, likely one of the children, reflects on their mother's ability to endure such emotional pain while maintaining her composure and dignity.

The poem explores the contrast between the mother's public image of strength and the internal struggles she faces. Despite the challenges she endures within her own family, she remains a pillar of strength and love in the eyes of the community.

The speaker expresses a sense of awe and admiration for their mother's ability to keep her emotions hidden, pondering the secret behind her unwavering resolve. The mother's resilience becomes a source of inspiration, symbolizing the quiet strength that lies within her.

Ultimately, the poem reflects on the complexity of human emotions and the depth of a mother's love, even in the face of adversity. It highlights the unspoken sacrifices and challenges that mothers often face, offering a poignant tribute to their enduring strength and love.

Poem

The Strength in Silence

In the face of strife, I find my strength,
Silent resolve, a shield at length.
Though taunted and torn, I hold my tongue,
For in silence, my defiance is flung.

Words may wound, but silence is might,
A steadfast refuge in the fight.
When faced with scorn, I choose restraint,
For silence speaks where words might taint.

In every battle, both big and small,
Silence stands, unwavering through it all.
Against the storm of ridicule and scorn,
Silence prevails, a beacon reborn.

So let them jest and let them jeer,
My silence speaks what they can't hear.
For in the power of silence, I find my peace,
A strength that cannot easily cease.

Description:

This poem explores the empowering nature of silence in the face of adversity and conflict. The title, "The Strength in Silence," encapsulates the central theme of the poem, highlighting the resilience and fortitude found in the ability to remain silent amidst turmoil.

The verses delve into the speaker's experience of finding strength and resolve through silence. Despite being taunted and torn by words, the speaker chooses to hold their tongue, recognizing the power of silence as a form of defiance. Silence, in this context, becomes a shield against verbal attacks, allowing the speaker to maintain their composure and dignity.

The poem contrasts the fleeting impact of words, which may wound and taint, with the enduring strength of silence. In moments of conflict and ridicule, silence emerges as a steadfast refuge, offering a sense of calm and restraint amidst chaos.

Throughout the poem, silence is depicted as a beacon of resilience, standing unwaveringly against the storm of negativity and scorn. Despite the jests and jeers of others, the speaker's silence speaks volumes, conveying a sense of inner peace and unwavering strength.

Ultimately, "The Strength in Silence" celebrates the power of silence as a source of inner resilience and peace, highlighting its ability to transcend verbal conflicts and serve as a steadfast anchor in times of turmoil.

Poem

Gift of Life

In life's tender dance, where hope threads hang,
A plea frail, a table bare in shadows sang.
Flickers of light in the depths of night,
A hero rises, embodiment of light.

Blood type mismatched, a plea so free,
Hanging by hope in dire decree.
Through despair's dimness, a Savior's breath,
Unknown yet seen, the essence of life's depth.

A guardian unnamed, face in the haze,
Silent kindness in desperate days.
Grace's glimmer through shadows takes flight,
A donor emerges, breathing life into night.

Debt owed to the silent, their compassion's role,
Gift of life, a grace-filled symphony, whole.
In fate's opera, a silent crescendo,
An eternal friend, a hero, though unknown.

Anonymous yet forever sung,
In gratitude's ballad, heartstrings strung.
To the stranger who lent life's vital hue,
Forever thankful, a debt owed to you.

Description:

This poem, titled "The Gift of Life: An Ode to an Unknown Hero," beautifully captures the profound gratitude and reverence for an anonymous donor who saves a life. The verses depict a poignant narrative of desperation and hope, where a plea for help hangs in the balance of despair.

In the depths of darkness, a hero emerges, their face obscured yet their kindness radiant. The imagery of grace's glimmer and the silent crescendo of fate's opera evoke a sense of awe and wonder at the selfless act of giving life.

The poem celebrates the unnamed donor as an eternal friend and hero, forever sung in gratitude's ballad. It speaks to the debt owed to this silent saviour, whose compassion and generosity breathe vitality into the night.

Each stanza resonates with a profound sense of appreciation and indebtedness to the stranger who, through their selfless act, bestows the precious gift of life upon another.

Poem

Everlasting Love:
A Tribute to Motherhood

In you, dear mother, I found my loyal friend,
Your love, my first, will echo to the end.
Adored by all who gazed upon your grace,
Your children's hearts, your love did embrace.

Not just by humans, but nature's kin too,
Animals, plants, and trees found solace in you.
With every smile, a magic spell was cast,
Enchanting hearts, a love that forever lasts.

Your gentle voice, a melody so sweet,
Could beckon cows and horses from their retreat.
Connected to the world in ways unseen,
A bond with nature, profound and serene.

Description:

My mother is depicted as a figure of immense love, loyalty, and connection to the world around her. She was not only cherished by her children but also by everyone who encounters her. Her love extends beyond human relationships to encompass animals, plants, and the natural world, demonstrating a deep empathy and compassion.

Her smile is described as magical, capable of captivating hearts and drawing others towards her. Even her voice held a special power, able to summon animals from afar, showcasing her harmonious relationship with nature.

As for me, the poem suggests a profound admiration and love for my mother. I recognise her as my most loyal friend and my first love, highlighting the special bond between a mother and her child. Through my words, it's evident that mother's presence in my life brings comfort, joy, and a sense of belonging.

Poem

Silent Tears

*Mother, I watched in silence as tears fell from your eyes,
Unable to ease your pain, my heart heavy with sighs.
I longed to wipe away each tear, to see you smile anew,
But as a child, I felt helpless, not knowing what to do.*

*Your silent weeping spoke volumes, though no words were spoken,
Each tear a testament to the pain you silently bore, unbroken.
I wished to be a comforting embrace, a source of solace near,
To chase away the shadows, to banish every fear.*

*But in my innocence, I thought tears were signs of woe,
Not realizing they could heal, allowing emotions to flow.
So, I watched you weep in silence, my heart breaking in two,
Yearning to bring you comfort, to lighten burdens you knew.*

*Now as I reflect on those moments, memories bittersweet,
I wish I could turn back time, our bond to truly meet.
Mother, your tears taught me empathy, compassion deep,
In every silent weeping, a love eternal, to forever keep.*

Description:

In the detailed description of the poem, we delve into the poignant relationship between the speaker and their mother, focusing on the mother's silent tears and the impact it had on the speaker as they grew up.

The poem captures the speaker's observations of their mother's silent weeping, portraying a scene where the mother is visibly distressed yet chooses to express her pain in silence. This silence becomes a profound language of its own, speaking volumes to the speaker even without words being uttered. The mother's tears symbolize the struggles and hardships she faces, which remain hidden from the world but deeply felt by her child.

As the speaker witnesses their mother's tears, they experience a mixture of emotions. They feel a sense of helplessness, unable to offer comfort or solace to alleviate their mother's pain. Instead, they carry a heavy burden of sorrow, feeling the weight of their mother's tears as if it were their own. The sight of their mother's tears pierces their heart, causing it to ache with empathy and longing to bring relief.

Despite their inability to ease their mother's suffering, the speaker's love, and admiration for her shine through in every line of the poem. They recognize the strength and resilience embodied in their mother's silent tears, admiring her ability to persevere through hardships while maintaining grace and dignity. The speaker's desire to see their mother smile again reflects a deep-rooted bond and an unwavering commitment to her well-being.

Overall, the poem portrays a tender and profound connection between the speaker and their mother, defined by empathy, love, and a shared understanding of silent struggles. It highlights the complexities of maternal relationships and the enduring impact of a mother's tears on her child's heart.

Poem

Echoes of Hop

*In a world where shadows loom,
Despair consumes, and darkness gloom.
Where beauty fades, and hearts are torn,
Injustice reigns, and hope is worn.*

*Yet amidst the chaos and the strife,
A whisper lingers, a thread of life.
Echoes of hope in the silent night,
A beacon shining, burning bright.*

*For though the road is rough and steep,
And tears may fall, and wounds may seep,
There's still a chance for love to rise,
To pierce the darkness, reach the skies.*

*In every act of kindness shown,
In every heart that's not alone,
There lies the seed of hope's embrace,
A promise of a brighter place.*

*So let us hold on to this light,
And banish darkness from our sight.
For in the depths of human soul,
Echoes of hope will make us whole.*

Description:

This poem delves into the paradoxical natsure of the human experience, juxtaposing themes of despair and hope within the context of a world filled with injustice and moral decay. The verses paint a somber picture of a society where beauty is overshadowed by ugliness, and where values like love, respect, and loyalty are eroded by selfishness and apathy.

The title, "Echoes of Hope," encapsulates the underlying message of resilience and the enduring potential for positive change. Despite the overwhelming challenges faced by humanity, there remains a flicker of hope, symbolized by the faint echoes reverberating through the darkness of despair.

The poem explores the struggle between darkness and light, acknowledging the pervasive influence of selfish desires and emotional detachment while also highlighting the inherent capacity for empathy and compassion to break through the barriers of apathy.

Ultimately, "Echoes of Hope" serves as a reminder that, even in the face of adversity, there is still the possibility for love and kindness to thrive, offering a glimmer of light in the darkest of times.

Walking the Path of Loss

On this winding road where sorrow lies,
Twists and turns, veiled by tear-filled eyes.
A sea of grief, tumultuous and wild,
Waves of pain, like an unwelcome child.

Yet within our tears, courage takes a stand,
Strength emerges, hand in hand.
Hope's ember, deep in the heart, aglow,
Guiding us through the ebb and flow.

Resilient spirits intertwine,
Walking together, yours and mine.
Through the journey, hand in hand,
Grief may linger, but love withstands.

Description:

In "Walking the Path of Loss," the journey of grief is depicted as a winding road filled with sorrow and tears. The poem portrays the tumultuous emotions experienced when facing loss, likening them to waves of pain that seem relentless. Despite the overwhelming grief, there is a glimmer of courage that emerges, offering strength to navigate the difficult terrain. Hope, symbolized as an ember in the heart, provides guidance through the ups and downs of the grieving process.

The poem emphasizes the interconnectedness of individuals in their grief journey, highlighting the importance of companionship and support. Together, resilient spirits walk hand in hand, facing the challenges of loss united. While grief may linger, the enduring power of love prevails, offering solace and comfort along the way.

Poem

Golden Mother, Endless Light

In the sky's colourful arch, a sight so divine,
There lies a treasure, a mother so fine.
Like gold at the end of the rainbow's bright hue,
Your love shines through, ever pure and true.

With every storm and every tear,
You're the beacon of hope, always near.
Guiding us through life's trials and pain,
Your love, like gold, will always remain.

Through highs and lows, you're our guiding light,
A source of strength, shining so bright.
In your arms, we find solace and peace,
Your love, like gold, will never cease.

So, here's to you, our dear mother so dear,
Your love, like gold, forever clear.
At the end of the rainbow, you'll always be,
The greatest treasure for eternity.

Description:

In the poem, "You are the gold at the end of the rainbow, mother," the imagery of a rainbow symbolizes hope, beauty, and the promise of better days ahead. By likening the mother to the gold at the end of the rainbow, it portrays her as a rare and precious treasure, one that brings joy, comfort, and fulfillment to those around her.

The detailed description of the mother as the gold at the end of the rainbow emphasizes her unique and invaluable qualities. She is depicted as a source of light and warmth in times of darkness, just like the golden glow that illuminates the sky at the rainbow's end. Her love is portrayed as enduring and unwavering, symbolizing the timeless and priceless nature of her bond with her children.

Furthermore, the comparison to gold highlights the mother's strength, resilience, and worth. Gold is often associated with purity, value, and rarity, echoing the exceptional qualities of the mother's love and character. Like gold, she is cherished, treasured, and held in high esteem by those who are fortunate enough to know her.

Overall, the poem pays tribute to the mother's profound impact and importance in the lives of her children. She is not just a parent but a guiding force, a source of inspiration, and a beacon of hope. Through her love and presence, she brings light and beauty into the world, just like the gold at the end of the rainbow.

Poem

In Life's Guiding Embrace

In the theater of existence, life unfolds its plan,
A compassionate mentor, guiding every woman and man.
Wisdom not from manuals, but experiences we embrace,
In the intricate dance of time, life leaves its trace.

Heartbeats echo wisdom, the seconds wisely tell,
As moments unfurl, stories of joy and farewell.
Life and time, a duet in the grand play,
Each interaction teaches, in its unique way.

Life whispers secrets, through laughter and tears,
Time's steady heartbeat, echoing the years.
From the cradle to the twilight chime,
The intertwined dance of life and time.

Value in moments, not just the ticking clock,
A symphony of teachings in every tick and tock.
So, in this waltz, with steps often prime,
We learn the dance of life and the melody of time."

Description:

"In Life's Guiding Embrace" is a profound exploration of life's journey, likening it to a theatrical performance where everyone plays a unique role. Life is portrayed as a compassionate mentor, guiding, and shaping the experiences of every person. The poem emphasizes that true wisdom comes not from textbooks but from the experiences we encounter and embrace along the way.

The imagery of heartbeats and the passage of time symbolize the rhythm of life, with each moment serving as a lesson in the grand play of existence. Joy and sorrow are intertwined, and each interaction teaches valuable lessons, contributing to the growth and understanding of individuals.

The poem highlights the importance of cherishing every moment and finding value in the experiences themselves, rather than simply counting the passing of time. It encourages readers to listen to the whispers of life, which speak through laughter and tears, and to appreciate the steady heartbeat of time, which echoes the passage of years.

Ultimately, "In Life's Guiding Embrace" reminds us that life is a dance, with each step carrying its own significance and each moment contributing to the melody of our existence. Through this dance, we learn, grow, and find meaning in the ever-unfolding journey of life.

Poem

Serenade of Love

In the realm above, a divine gift unfurls,
An angelic mother, in love's eternal swirl.
Cherished moments, forever embraced,
Her heart, where love finds a sacred space.

Selfless toil for her children's care,
Bearing unseen burdens with grace so rare.
Labors profound, unknown to the crowd,
Prayers, tears, and nights profound.

Reasons for living, pure and bright,
To witness children's joy, happiness ignite.
Encounters etched in memory's glow,
A heartfelt slideshow of joy and woe.

Heart aches, reliving scenes so dear,
Pages turning, moments crystal clear.
Little finger yearns for a touch so divine,
Heart longs for connection, in love's design.

At the table, echoes of feeding hands,
Grown-up, carried horsey-back across lands.
Playing like children, love fully deployed,
Childhood memories forever enjoyed.

Inspiration, mentor, confidant so near,
Heartbeat, friend, wiping every tear.
In the symphony of life, she played a part,
A serenade of love, eternally in our heart.

Description:

"Serenade of Love" paints a poignant picture of the profound love and sacrifices made by a mother, elevated to angelic status in the eyes of her child. The poem captures the essence of maternal love as a divine gift, transcending earthly realms.

Each stanza evokes a sense of reverence and admiration for the mother's unwavering devotion to her children. She is depicted as a selfless figure, tirelessly labouring for their well-being and shouldering unseen burdens with grace and dignity. Her love creates a sacred space in her heart, where cherished moments with her children are forever embraced.

The poem delves into the reasons for living, highlighting the joy that comes from witnessing her children's happiness and the profound impact of shared encounters. Memories, both joyful and sorrowful, are etched in the heart, forming a heartfelt slideshow of life's journey.

Throughout the verses, there is a yearning for connection and a longing for the touch of a mother's hand, even as time passes and children grow. The imagery of childhood memories, such as feeding hands and horsey-back rides, brings nostalgia and warmth, reminding readers of the enduring bond between mother and child.

The mother is portrayed as an inspiration, mentor, and confidant, always present to wipe away tears and share in life's joys and sorrows. Her role in the symphony of life is likened to a serenade of love, resonating eternally in the hearts of her children. Overall, "Serenade of Love" celebrates the timeless and unconditional love of a mother, a love that remains steadfast and unwavering through the passage of time.

Hope Amidst Chaos

In this world so fair, we find despair,
Where beauty fades in a world unfair.
People misuse, tarnish the name,
Of God's creation, tainted by shame.

Morals and principles, lost in the throng,
As humanity stumbles, led blindly along.
Love, respect, and loyalty wane,
In a world where selfish desires reign.

Emotionless robots, devoid of care,
Crushing others, leaving hearts bare.
Self-serving needs, the only decree,
In a world where empathy struggles to be free.

Yet amidst the chaos, a glimmer remains,
Hope flickers softly, despite the strains.
For in the depths of human strife,
There's still the chance for love to thrive.

Description:

This poem "Hope Amidst Chaos" delves into the complexities of the human experience, painting a vivid picture of a world marred by despair and injustice. The verses explore the pervasive presence of selfishness and moral decay, where the values of love, respect, and loyalty are overshadowed by self-serving desires.

Despite the bleakness portrayed, there's a subtle undercurrent of optimism woven throughout the poem. The title, "Hope Amidst Chaos," encapsulates this theme of resilience and the enduring belief that, even in the darkest of times, there remains the possibility for love and compassion to prevail.

The poem highlights the dichotomy of the human condition, acknowledging the prevalent struggles while also acknowledging the potential for positive change and renewal. It serves as a reminder that, despite the challenges we face, hope is a powerful force that can guide us through even the most difficult of circumstances.

Poem

Mother hurried treasure

In her arms, a world of measure,
A mother, hurried, yet a treasure.
With love and care, she leads the way,
Guiding through each night and day.

Her hands, they work, her heart, it beats,
In every moment, her love repeats.
Through storms and trials, she stands tall,
Her love, a beacon, guiding all.

Though hurried, in her steps, a grace,
In every challenge, she finds her place.
A treasure, she, in every way,
A mother's love, come what may.

Description:

This poem paints a vivid picture of a mother who is always on the move, tending to her responsibilities with haste yet with a heart full of love and care. Despite the busyness of her life, she treasures every moment with her children, guiding them through life's challenges with grace and determination.

The phrase "hurried treasure" encapsulates the essence of this mother's role. She may be rushed in her actions, but she is a priceless gem to her children, providing them with love, guidance, and support at every turn. Her hurriedness is not a sign of neglect, but rather a testament to her dedication and commitment to her family.

In the midst of her bustling life, this mother's love shines through, illuminating the path for her children and nurturing them with tenderness and care. She is a treasure trove of wisdom, strength, and compassion, enriching the lives of those around her with her selfless devotion.

Overall, this poem celebrates the tireless efforts of mothers everywhere, acknowledging the invaluable role they play in shaping the lives of their children and the profound impact of their love and sacrifice.

Poem

Guiding Light

In the pages turned, my pain unveiled,
A book birthed, my story detailed.
You, my friend, the motivation's core,
Walked my shoes, understood even more.

Through impaired eyes, you stood so near,
Caring from afar, every doubt and fear.
Rest ensured, enough to eat,
Medication, appointments, tasks complete.

Sleepless nights, a book's quest pursued,
Health's turn harsh, in infection's mood.
Yet, you, the caring-natured guide,
Embarked when I was sinking, a turning tide.

Like mom, brother, and Alex, you became,
A great factor, not just in name.
My legacy lives on, thanks to you,
For being my eyes when sight withdrew.

Description:

"Guiding Light" delves into the intimate journey of the speaker, whose pain and struggles are unveiled within the pages of their life's story. The poem celebrates the profound impact of a dear friend who serves as a beacon of motivation and support, walking alongside the speaker through their darkest moments.

From the very beginning, the friend emerges as a source of strength and understanding, delving deep into the speaker's experiences, and empathizing with their pain. Despite physical distance, the friend's unwavering care and compassion provide solace and assurance, ensuring that the speaker's basic needs are met, and essential tasks are completed.

In moments of adversity, when health takes a turn for the worse, the friend remains a steadfast companion, offering guidance and support like a true family member. Their caring nature and selfless dedication shine through, offering hope and comfort to the speaker in their time of need.

Through the friend's unwavering presence and support, the speaker finds resilience and strength to navigate life's challenges, even in the face of adversity. Like a guiding light in the darkness, the friend illuminates the path forward, helping the speaker overcome obstacles and emerge triumphant.

Ultimately, the poem serves as a heartfelt tribute to the friend's enduring impact on the speaker's life. Their legacy lives on, not only in the tangible support they provide but also in the profound difference they make in the speaker's journey, serving as a guiding light through life's twists and turns.

Poem

Embracing Life's Canvas

In the tapestry of existence, do you see,
A thread of duties or a dance of opportunity?
Does life's weight crush or its wonders enthral?
The canvas of life, how do you view it all?

Fear not the journey, with doubts set free,
Scarcity's mindset, let it cease to be.
Through the twists and turns, don't be confined,
A life unexplored, a treasure to find.

No constant fears, let them dissipate,
Job insecurities, loneliness abate.
Failure and the unknown, a chance to grow,
Conflicts, embarrassments, let courage show.

Decisions challenging, embrace the strife,
Rejection, a part of a vibrant life.
Success, not a fear, but a welcomed quest,
Break free from fears, life at its best.

Description:

"Embracing Life's Canvas" invites readers to contemplate the myriad facets of existence and consider how they perceive life's journey. The poem encourages a shift in perspective from viewing life's challenges as burdensome duties to embracing them as opportunities for growth and exploration.

The opening lines prompt reflection on one's outlook on life, posing questions about whether one sees their responsibilities as burdensome threads in life's tapestry or as opportunities for joy and fulfillment. It challenges readers to examine whether they are weighed down by the challenges of life or inspired by its wonders.

As the poem unfolds, it urges readers to release themselves from the grip of fear and scarcity mindset, encouraging them to embrace life's uncertainties and possibilities. It advocates for a mindset of abundance and courage, urging readers to break free from the confines of their comfort zones and explore the richness of life.

The poem acknowledges the inevitability of challenges and setbacks but reframes them as opportunities for growth and learning. It encourages readers to face their fears head-on, viewing failures and rejections not as deterrents but as stepping stones on the path to success and fulfillment.

Ultimately, "Embracing Life's Canvas" is a call to action to approach life with courage, optimism, and resilience. It celebrates the vibrancy of life and encourages readers to break free from their fears and limitations, embracing the full spectrum of experiences that life has to offer.

The Beauty of life

In the tapestry of our days, a life's sweet song,
Beauty's melody in memories, lifelong.
Not just seen, but felt within the soul,
A dance of rarity, where moments unroll.

With years, a wisdom blooms so bright,
Rarity gleams in the softest light.
Amidst life's rubble, flowers take flight,
Whispers of beauty, soft and right.

Exultation found in lives well-lived,
Breathing easier, a gift we've sieved.
Inner peace, gratitude, purpose in tow,
Unveiling beauty, in every ebb and flow.

A way of seeing, reacting with grace,
Life's beauty unfolds in every space.
Moments divine, through any weather,
Harmony unveiled, woven threads together.

Description:

"The Beauty of Life" paints a vivid picture of the intricate tapestry of existence, where beauty is not merely observed but felt deeply within the soul. The poem celebrates the richness of life's experiences and the profound impact they have on shaping our perceptions and memories.

As the poem unfolds, it highlights the transformative power of wisdom that comes with age, illuminating the rare and precious moments that shimmer in the softest light amidst life's challenges. Through the metaphor of flowers taking flight amidst rubble, the poem captures the essence of resilience and the capacity for beauty to emerge even in the most unexpected places.

The verses exalt the joy and fulfillment that accompany a life well-lived, where inner peace, gratitude, and purpose become guiding beacons through the journey of existence. Each moment is imbued with beauty, whether in times of ease or adversity, revealing the intricate interplay of light and shadow that defines the human experience.

The poem champions a way of seeing that embraces grace and appreciation for the beauty that surrounds us, even in the face of life's storms. It evokes a sense of harmony and interconnectedness, where every thread in life's tapestry weaves together to create a symphony of experiences that resonate with the soul.

Poem

The Gift of Life:
An Ode to an Unknown Hero

In life's tender dance, where hope threads hang,
A plea frail, a table bare in shadows sang.
Flickers of light in the depths of night,
A hero rises, embodiment of light.

Blood type mismatched, a plea so free,
Hanging by hope in dire decree.
Through despair's dimness, a Savior's breath,
Unknown yet seen, the essence of life's depth.

A guardian unnamed, face in the haze,
Silent kindness in desperate days.
Grace's glimmer through shadows takes flight,
A donor emerges, breathing life into night.

Debt owed to the silent, their compassion's role,
Gift of life, a grace-filled symphony, whole.
In fate's opera, a silent crescendo,
An eternal friend, a hero, though unknown.

Anonymous yet forever sung,
In gratitude's ballad, heartstrings strung.
To the stranger who lent life's vital hue,
Forever thankful, a debt owed to you.

Description:

"In the Shadows of Compassion" "The Gift of Life: An Ode to an Unknown Hero" delves into the poignant narrative of a plea for life amidst the darkness of despair, where hope hangs by a fragile thread. The poem portrays the stark contrast between the dire circumstances faced by the protagonist and the flickers of light that pierce through the depths of despair.

At the heart of the poem lies the embodiment of light and salvation, a hero who emerges from the shadows to offer a lifeline in the form of a life-saving donation. Despite the mismatched blood type and the bleakness of the situation, the hero's silent kindness shines through, breathing new life into the darkness.

The verses evoke a sense of awe and gratitude towards the unnamed guardian whose compassionate act transcends words. Their selfless gesture becomes a beacon of hope in the face of adversity, a silent crescendo in fate's opera that transforms despair into a symphony of grace.

Through the narrative, the poem pays homage to the anonymous hero, forever sung in the ballad of gratitude. Their act of compassion becomes a testament to the power of human kindness and the profound impact it can have on the lives of others. In the end, the poem serves as a heartfelt expression of gratitude to the stranger who bestowed the gift of life, forever indebted to their silent yet profound act of compassion.

Poem

Love's Radiance: A Valentine's Day Celebration

On this special day, Valentine's bright,
Let joy and love fill the morning light.
May hearts be lifted, spirits soar,
As love's embrace knocks on each door.

To all who labour, to all who strive,
You're cherished on this day, so alive.
With every smile, with every cheer,
Feel the warmth of love draw near.

In every task, in every goal,
Find love's essence, make it whole.
For in the bonds that we create,
Love's radiance can never abate.

Though shadows may linger, and doubts may rise,
Know that love sees through disguise.
In the tapestry of life, your thread is true,
So, embrace this day, let love shine through.

With every beat, with every rhyme,
May you feel love's touch, for all time.
For on this day, Valentine's so grand,
Let love's light guide you hand in hand.

Description:

This poem celebrates the essence of Valentine's Day, radiating warmth, joy, and love. It sets the scene for a day filled with positivity and affection, inviting readers to embrace the morning light and the spirit of love. The poem acknowledges the efforts and struggles of everyone, emphasizing that they are valued and appreciated on this special day.

Each stanza conveys a message of love and appreciation, encouraging readers to recognize the beauty in their connections with others. It emphasizes the importance of love in overcoming challenges and finding fulfillment in life's endeavors.

The imagery evoked in the poem paints a picture of a day infused with love, where every smile and every gesture is filled with genuine affection. It encourages readers to cherish the bonds they have created and to let love guide them through life's journey.

Overall, the poem captures the essence of Valentine's Day as a time to celebrate love in all its forms and to bask in the warmth of heartfelt connections. It serves as a reminder to embrace love, both giving and receiving, on this special day and beyond.

Poem

Harmony of Hearts

In my chest, a blend of hues so bright
A crazy mix, cheeky, wild, and right.
Moment's tender, a touch both soft and rough,
Velvet smooth, elixir of love's sweet stuff.

In love's fusion, a unique affair,
A breath of freshness beyond compare.
You, my sunshine divine and rare,
Souls entwined, envy's distant glare.

Hey, hey! O luckiest, don't you see?
Between my verses, it's you and me.
Heart and love, a treasure vast,
Each joy cherished, moments that last.

Laughter echoes, lessons strong,
In love's dance, where we belong.
Through life's waves, together we stand,
Challenges conquered, hand in hand.

Ku'u aloha, thank you, so sincere,
Loving you more, with each passing year.
Hey! Every fiber yearns, a heartfelt burn,
In the echoes of my heart, your name's return.

Description:

"In Love's Melody" "Harmony of Hearts" intricately weaves together the colours and textures of a profound love story, painting a vivid picture of the bond shared between two souls. The poem captures the essence of love's myriad hues, blending cheekiness, wildness, and tenderness into a harmonious fusion.

Each moment is depicted as a delicate blend of softness and roughness, akin to velvet smoothness, infused with the elixir of love's sweet essence. The love shared between the speaker and their beloved is portrayed as a unique and enchanting affair, characterized by freshness and depth beyond comparison.

The verses exude a sense of joy and gratitude for the presence of the beloved, described as a divine and rare sunshine that brightens the speaker's world. Their souls are depicted as entwined, shielded from the envy of onlookers, as they navigate life's journey together with unwavering love and companionship.

The poem celebrates the shared experiences and cherished moments between the speaker and their beloved, highlighting the laughter, lessons, and strong bond that define their relationship. Despite the challenges they face, they stand united, conquering obstacles hand in hand, with a deep sense of gratitude and sincerity towards each other.

The closing lines express a heartfelt yearning and burning passion for the beloved, their name echoing in the chambers of the speaker's heart with each beat. It is a testament to the enduring power of love, which grows stronger with each passing year, enriching the lives of those who are fortunate enough to experience its embrace.

Poem

A Haven Within

Grant me, oh Lord, Your gaze so divine,
To perceive each twist, every design.
May Your voice weave a melody sweet,
Guiding my steps in life's rhythmic beat.

In the intricate dance of choices we face,
Let discernment shine, truth's steady embrace.
Your wisdom, a lamp in shadows' deep,
I declare Your direction, my soul to keep.

Through the toughest moments, my heart steadfast,
On You, my Rock, a refuge to last.
Salvation's song echoes within my soul,
Life's cornerstone, making me whole.

In Your embrace, solace profound I find,
A shelter in storms, grace unconfined.
Eternal refuge in Your love so vast,
On You, my Rock, a refuge to last.

Description:

"A Haven Within" tenderly invokes a plea to the divine for guidance, solace, and refuge amidst life's complexities and challenges. The poem begins with a heartfelt request for the divine gaze, seeking the ability to perceive the intricate twists and designs of life's journey. The speaker longs for the divine voice to weave a melody of guidance, leading their steps in harmony with life's rhythmic beat.

As choices abound and challenges arise, the speaker invokes the presence of divine discernment, recognizing the steady embrace of truth and wisdom. The divine wisdom is likened to a lamp in the shadows, offering direction and illumination in moments of uncertainty.

Throughout the verses, the speaker expresses steadfast faith and reliance on the divine as their Rock and refuge. Even in the toughest moments, the speaker's heart remains unwavering, finding solace and salvation in the embrace of the divine presence. The divine love is portrayed as an eternal refuge, offering grace unconfined and making the speaker feel whole.

Ultimately, "A Haven Within" celebrates the profound sense of peace and security found in the divine embrace. It serves as a heartfelt acknowledgment of the divine's role as a steadfast anchor amidst life's storms, providing refuge and solace that endures beyond the passage of time.

Poem

A Heart's Surrender

In humble gratitude, my voice ascends,
To the divine, beneath the sky that extends.
Blessings fall like gentle rain's embrace,
I bow before You, in this sacred space.

Forgiveness sought for burdens I bear,
In Your mercy, solace rare and fair.
My strength, my life's unwavering foundation,
I surrender all, a sacred declaration.

Spirit cleanse, let purity gently flow,
Heal wounds from long ago.
In the echoes of forgiving grace,
My heart finds peace, a sacred embrace.

Guide me, oh Light, through the darkest night,
In Your love, shadows take their flight.
Family, friends, and even my foes,
Wrap them in love that eternally glows.

To Your love, celestial and tireless,
A flame that in my soul inspires.
In this prayer, my soul extends,
Gratitude and forgiveness, where life transcends."

Description:

"A Heart's Surrender" delves into the depths of human experience, offering a poignant portrayal of gratitude, forgiveness, and spiritual connection. The poem begins with a humble acknowledgment of the divine presence, expressed through a voice that ascends in gratitude beneath the expansive sky.

Blessings are likened to gentle rain, enveloping the speaker in a comforting embrace, evoking a sense of reverence as they bow before the divine in a sacred space. Seeking forgiveness for burdens carried, the speaker finds solace in the mercy and grace bestowed upon them, acknowledging the divine as the unwavering foundation of their strength and life.

The poem delves into themes of purification and healing, as the spirit is cleansed and wounds of the past are tended to with gentle care. Through the echoes of forgiving grace, the speaker's heart finds peace, embracing forgiveness as a sacred act of liberation.

Guided by the light of divine love, the speaker navigates through the darkest nights, finding solace and courage in the shadows' retreat. The sentiment extends beyond personal healing, encompassing family, friends, and even foes, wrapping them in the eternal glow of love and forgiveness.

Ultimately, the poem celebrates the tireless and celestial nature of divine love, which serves as a source of inspiration and guidance for the speaker's soul. In this prayerful surrender, gratitude and forgiveness intertwine, offering a transcendent glimpse into the boundless depths of the human spirit.

Poem

Harmony Within

*Within the mirror's gaze, self-love unfolds,
A resilient bond, like nature's stories told.
Trust, a fortress deep in my very core,
Challenges embraced, each explored.*

*Foolish pursuit of external delight,
For within resides the true love's light.
No other's affection can truly compare,
In solitude's grace, my strength is laid bare.*

*God's love, a beacon, pure and divine,
Guiding with grace, like stars that shine.
In the dance of self-discovery, I find,
A profound love forever intertwined.*

Description:

"Harmony Within" tenderly explores the journey of self-love and discovery, celebrating the resilient bond found within oneself. The poem begins by acknowledging the unfolding of self-love within the reflection of the mirror, likening it to the timeless stories told by nature. Trust is depicted as a fortress deep within the speaker's core, allowing them to embrace life's challenges with courage and resilience.

The poem contrasts the fleeting pursuit of external delights with the enduring light of self-love that resides within. The speaker recognizes that true affection cannot be found elsewhere, as their strength and grace are revealed in moments of solitude.

The divine presence is invoked as a beacon of pure love and guidance, akin to the stars that illuminate the night sky. In the journey of self-discovery, the speaker finds a profound love that is forever intertwined with their being, leading to a harmonious relationship with oneself and the divine.

Poem

Echoes of Serenity

'Midst the world's tumult, a chorus in strife,
Sits the Serene One, architect of life.
Amid demands' wild sway, emotions' array,
Unmoved, the Tranquil One whispers at dawn, in tranquillity lay.

Grant strength, Lord, to calm the raging seas,
Purify the dwelling of Your divine keys.
A thousand voices seek recognition,
Yet within chaos, the One's silence, divine mission.

Bustling deals and cries ceaseless,
In life's hustle, discern silent ties that bless.
Where one concern prevails, undivided attention,
Hearing Your voice, in quiet surrender's ascension.

"Lord, with whips of Your zeal, cleanse the core,
Fill me with singular concern, forevermore.
Grant a mind attuned to Your wisdom's song,
A will devoted, blessed stillness lifelong.

Description:

"Echoes of Serenity" paints a vivid picture of the tranquillity found amidst life's chaos, with the Serene One serving as the guiding force. The poem captures the essence of seeking solace and strength from the divine amidst the turmoil of daily life.

The Serene One is depicted as the architect of life, unaffected by the wild sway of demands and emotions that characterize human existence. Instead, their presence whispers of tranquillity, offering a sense of peace and calmness that transcends the noise of the world.

The speaker's prayer for strength to calm the raging seas and purify their soul reflects a longing for divine intervention in the midst of life's challenges. Amidst the clamor of a thousand voices seeking recognition, the silence of the Serene One's divine mission stands out, reminding the speaker of the power of quietude amidst chaos.

The poem emphasizes the importance of discerning silent ties that bless amidst life's bustling deals and ceaseless cries. In the hustle and bustle of life, the speaker seeks undivided attention to hear the divine voice and surrender to its guidance.

Ultimately, the prayer for cleansing and devotion reflects a desire for a mind attuned to divine wisdom and a will devoted to blessed stillness. "Echoes of Serenity" invites readers to find refuge in the quiet surrender to the divine amidst life's cacophony.

Poem

Blessed in Affection

*Lucky to have you, my love so sweet,
Cherishing moments, hearts wildly beat.
In you, my friend forever found,
 A love story with no bounds.*

*Imagine life without you, inconceivable,
With you, each day feels unbelievable.
You're amazing, my dear, beyond compare,
Waking up beside you, a dream so rare.*

*Everything right, my joy, my pride,
In your love, eternally I confide.
Lucky to find you, forever intertwined,
Your presence in my heart, magnificently enshrined.*

*Love echoes, sweet and vibrant refrain,
In my heart, forever it shall sustain.
Together we stand, our spirits linger,
Forever entwined, touched by your finger.*

*Here's to us, to love so true,
A journey together, just me and you.
In your love, I've found my art,
Forever and always, you're in my heart.*

Description:

"Blessed in Affection" is a heartfelt ode to the deep and enduring love shared between the speaker and their beloved. The poem beautifully captures the essence of gratitude and admiration for the cherished bond they share.

The opening lines express the speaker's profound appreciation for their beloved, describing them as a source of sweetness and joy in their life. The love shared between them is portrayed as a treasure beyond measure, with hearts beating wildly in celebration of their connection.

The speaker reflects on the invaluable friendship found in their beloved, emphasizing the depth and boundlessness of their love story. Imagining life without their beloved is deemed inconceivable, as each day with them feels unbelievably precious and fulfilling.

The poem celebrates the uniqueness and incomparable qualities of the beloved, describing them as amazing and beyond compare. Waking up beside them is likened to a dream, highlighting the rare and exceptional nature of their love.

Throughout the verses, there is a sense of joy, pride, and unwavering trust in the love shared between the speaker and their beloved. Their love is depicted as a constant presence, magnificently enshrined in the speaker's heart and soul.

The poem concludes with a toast to their enduring love, symbolizing a commitment to journey through life together, hand in hand. The love shared between the speaker and their beloved is portrayed as a timeless and everlasting bond, forever cherished and celebrated in the depths of the speaker's heart.

Poem

Whispers of Affection

In my world, your words dawn like the sun,
Brushing joy with hues, a love that's never done.
Melodic messages echo in my heart's domain,
Composing a symphony, a blissful refrain.

Wrapped in the warmth of your love's embrace,
Each waking moment, a beautiful grace.
Sweet sentiments dive into my soul's deep,
Creating smiles, thoughts of you to keep.

Your love, a treasure pure and sincere,
Clasped tightly, my heart holds it near.
The ache of missing finds solace in your presence,
Expressions of love unveil our connection's essence.

"Blessed be the womb," your words resonate,
Echoing love, our intertwined fate.
In the silent dance of thoughts, minds align,
Hearts beating to a rhythm, love so divine.

Though distances linger, love spans wide,
To the moon and back, a forever guide.
Wishing your day bathed in warmth and cheer,
As you've generously poured into mine, my dear.

Description:

"Whispers of Affection" tenderly captures the essence of love through the delicate interplay of words and emotions. The poem portrays the speaker's deep appreciation for their beloved's words and the profound impact they have on their life.

The opening lines liken the arrival of the beloved's words to the dawn of a new day, infusing joy and color into the speaker's world. The love shared between them is depicted as a continuous journey, never-ending and always evolving.

As the verses unfold, the poem delves into the intimate connection shared between the speaker and their beloved. The warmth of the beloved's love envelops the speaker, gracing each moment with beauty and grace. Sweet sentiments from the beloved penetrate the depths of the speaker's soul, eliciting smiles and filling their thoughts with thoughts of love.

The poem celebrates the purity and sincerity of the beloved's love, highlighting its significance in the speaker's life. Despite the ache of missing their beloved, the speaker finds solace in their presence and the profound connection they share.

The verses resonate with the echo of love's enduring bond, intertwining fate, and aligning minds and hearts. Even in the face of distance, love knows no bounds, spanning wide and serving as a guiding light through life's journey.

In the final lines, the speaker extends warm wishes to their beloved, expressing gratitude for the love and warmth they bring into their life. The poem concludes with a heartfelt acknowledgment of the beloved's generosity and the profound impact they have on the speaker's life.

Poem

The Tapestry of Time

In the vast loom of existence, a truth unfolds,
"The Tapestry of Time," where stories are told.
Everything arrives, a melody in its own rhyme,
In the right time, orchestrated by the divine.

Trust in the maker, the creator's grand plan,
A cosmic dance, guided by a steady hand.
Patience, a virtue, a whisper in the breeze,
As life's tapestry weaves destinies with ease.

Be grateful for each thread, each moment spun,
In the grand design, where all is begun.
For every twist and turn, each stitch so fine,
Adds depth and beauty to the grand design divine.

In the tapestry of time, our lives intertwine,
Threads of love and hope, forever align.
With each passing moment, the pattern unfolds,
A masterpiece of stories, ancient and bold.

Description:

"The Tapestry of Time" is a poetic exploration of life's journey and the interconnectedness of all things in the universe. It begins by metaphorically portraying existence as a vast loom where the fabric of time is woven, with each thread representing a unique story or experience. This imagery evokes a sense of awe and wonder at the complexity and beauty of life's tapestry.

The poem emphasizes the idea that everything happens in its own time, according to a divine plan orchestrated by a higher power. It encourages trust in this plan and advocates for patience as we navigate the twists and turns of life. The mention of "a whisper in the breeze" suggests a gentle reminder to stay grounded and present, even amidst life's challenges.

As the verses progress, the poem invites reflection on gratitude for every moment and experience, recognizing the significance of each thread in the overall design of life. It celebrates the intricacies of existence and encourages appreciation for the interconnectedness of all beings.

The addition of the third verse expands on the theme of gratitude and acknowledges the importance of embracing life's complexities. It suggests that every twist and turn, every moment of joy or sorrow, contributes to the richness and depth of the tapestry of life.

The final verse further emphasizes the interconnected nature of human experience, highlighting the bonds of love and hope that unite us all. It portrays life as an ongoing process of discovery and creation, where each moment adds to the unfolding masterpiece of our collective story.

Overall, "The Tapestry of Time" invites readers to contemplate the beauty and complexity of life, encouraging them to embrace every moment with gratitude and humility.

Poem

Life's Priceless Treasure

In life's grand tapestry, silver may gleam,
And fortunes may rise, as if in a dream.
But amidst the riches, one truth prevails,
Life's value, unmatched, never pales.

For silver may shine, but it can't compare,
To the breath in our lungs, the love we share.
God's blessings abound, in every way,
Yet life's precious gift, beyond all sway.

In the grand scheme of things, we come to see,
That life's true worth is boundlessly free.
So cherish each moment, with love in your heart,
For life's priceless treasure, is where we start.

Detailed Description:

This poem priceless treasure eloquently captures the essence of life's true value amidst the allure of material wealth and worldly success. The imagery of silver gleaming and fortunes rising highlights the external markers of success and abundance. However, the poem reminds us that true richness lies beyond material possessions.

The repetition of the phrase "Life's value, unmatched, never pales" emphasizes the central theme of the poem – the incomparable worth of life itself. Despite the transient nature of worldly wealth, the poem asserts that the breath in our lungs and the love we share are invaluable treasures that far surpass material riches.

The poem acknowledges the abundance of blessings bestowed upon us by a higher power, yet it underscores that life's most precious gift cannot be bought or quantified. It is a reminder to cherish each moment and to hold love in our hearts as the most valuable asset.

Overall, "Life's Priceless Treasure" encourages gratitude for the gift of life and emphasizes the importance of living each moment with love and appreciation.

Sent from Above

Betrayed by friends, a storm in my life,
Sent from Above, a tale of pain and strife.
But in the tempest's rage, a beacon so bright,
A friend emerged, sent by celestial light.

Married, with a child, a life so full,
Yet through the chaos, he answered the call.
Two jobs, the weight of studies to bear,
Yet in the heavy traffic, he'd always be there.

No questions asked, no need for fame,
A genuine soul, not playing a game.
Respect, he'd offer, boss, in his tone,
Through the darkest times, I was not alone.

In a world that turned its back, he stood,
A rare gem, in the dense friendship wood.
Longtime companions, like shadows fled,
Betrayal's venom, where loyalty bled.

They ate my bread, drank from my cup,
Yet behind my back, deceit brewed up.
In my rainiest days, caused by their art,
They pushed me down, not playing a part.

But from the ashes, a friend arose,
Sent from above, where true friendship glows.
In his hand, a lifeline, strong and true,
With him by my side, I knew I'd pull through.

Description:

This poem tells the story of betrayal and resilience, highlighting the impact of friendship in times of adversity. The speaker describes being betrayed by friends, experiencing storms in life caused by deceit and betrayal. Despite the challenges faced, a beacon of light emerges in the form of a true friend, sent from above.

The friend described in the poem is depicted as a genuine soul, selflessly offering support and companionship during the speaker's darkest times. Despite juggling multiple responsibilities, including marriage, parenting, and work, this friend always makes time to be there for the speaker, even in heavy traffic. Their loyalty and genuine care stand in stark contrast to the deceit and betrayal experienced from other companions.

Through the trials and tribulations caused by betrayal, the speaker finds solace and strength in the unwavering support of this true friend. Their presence serves as a reminder of the power of genuine friendship to provide comfort, resilience, and hope in the face of adversity.

Overall, "Sent from Above" celebrates the transformative power of true friendship, emphasizing its ability to uplift and support us during life's storms and challenges. It acknowledges the pain of betrayal while also highlighting the healing and redemptive nature of genuine companionship sent from above.

Poem

True Friendship's Glow

In moments dark when shadows loomed,
And trust betrayed, my heart consumed,
A friend emerged, a shining light,
Guiding me through the darkest night.

When family faltered, turned away,
And friends betrayed, led me astray,
This loyal soul, unwavering, true,
Stood by my side, saw me through.

Their presence, like a beacon bright,
Dispelled the shadows, brought new light,
In times of need, they never waned,
A steadfast ally forever gained.

Through trials faced and battles fought,
Their friendship, a treasure dearly sought,
With kindness, love, and empathy,
They healed my wounds and set me free.

So here's to the friend who stood by me,
In moments when others couldn't see,
Their loyalty, a gift so rare,
A bond we'll cherish, beyond compare.

Detailed Description:

Maduike Sampson, a Nigerian-born individual living in Australia, exemplifies dedication and selflessness in serving the community at large. As a best-of-the-best friend and work colleague, Maduike's commitment to supporting others is evident in every aspect of his life. Despite the challenges he faces, including balancing a marriage, fatherhood, multiple jobs, and studies, Maduike remains steadfast in his dedication to those around him. His genuine sincerity, unwavering support, and respectful demeanor set him apart as a rare gem in the friendship circle, shining brightly even in the darkest of times. Maduike's resilience in the face of betrayal and deceit speaks volumes about his character, as he emerges stronger and more determined to uphold the values of true friendship and loyalty.

To Maduike Sampson, your unwavering dedication to serving others and your steadfast commitment to friendship inspire us all. In the face of adversity, you shine as a beacon of light, reminding us of the power of genuine sincerity and resilience. Your presence in our lives is a blessing, and we are grateful for your unwavering support and friendship. Here's to you, Maduike, a true friend and a shining example of selflessness and dedication.

Poem dedicated to Maduike Sampson

True friendship glow is dedicated to a heartfelt poem dedicated to Maduike Sampson, born in Nigeria, and residing in Sydney, Australia. The verses evoke a sense of connection across continents, highlighting the unique journey that spans from the Southern Hemisphere to the Northern Hemisphere. The imagery of Sydney's Southern Cross and Nigeria's North Star symbolizes the global embrace of Maduike's experiences. The poem is a celebration of the interconnectedness of lives across vast distances and the shared human experiences that transcend geographical boundaries. The title, the true friendship glow encapsulates the essence of the dedication, emphasizing the subtl connection and communication that exists across the diverse landscapes of our world.

Poem

Wings of Self-Belief

In the vast expanse, a mantra unfolds,
"Wings of Self-Belief," a story to be told.
A bird on a branch, a metaphor profound,
Trust not in the branch, but in wings unbound.

Perched on life's tree, branches may sway,
Yet, fearless she sits, come what may.
Her trust lies not in the fragile bough,
But in the strength of wings, here and now.

A lesson profound, a truth to share,
Believe in yourself, the currents dare.
In the flight of dreams, soar, and sing,
For in self-belief, you find your wing.

Description:

"Wings of Self-Belief" is a captivating exploration of inner strength and resilience, depicted through the metaphor of a bird perched on a branch. The poem invites readers to reflect on the power of self-belief and the courage to trust in one's own abilities, even in the face of uncertainty and adversity.

The opening lines introduce the central theme of the poem, presenting self-belief as a mantra that unfolds within the vast expanse of existence. This sets the stage for a story to be told, one that revolves around the transformative power of trust and confidence in oneself.

The imagery of a bird perched on a branch serves as a metaphor for the precarious nature of life's circumstances. Despite the branches swaying and the uncertainties of the world around her, the bird remains fearless and unwavering in her trust. This image conveys the idea that true strength lies not in external factors, but in the unwavering belief in one's own capabilities.

Through this metaphor, the poem imparts a profound lesson on the importance of self-belief and resilience in navigating life's challenges. It encourages readers to have faith in themselves and to embrace their inner strength, knowing that they have the power to soar above any obstacle.

Ultimately, "Wings of Self-Belief" inspires readers to cultivate a sense of confidence and trust in their own potential, reminding them that true freedom and fulfillment come from within. By believing in themselves and embracing their unique gifts, individuals can unlock the power to pursue their dreams and reach new heights of personal growth and achievement.

Poem

Mother's Love, a Sacred Vine

What was it like, Mother dear,
To carry me, your heart so near?
Conceiving me, what thoughts entwined,
In the sacred chamber of your mind?

Was I a dream, a love so pure,
In your embrace, forever secure?
A journey shared, a bond divine,
As you felt my first flutter, the subtle sign.

Amidst life's hustle, roles to play,
Did you find moments to love, to sway?
In the chaos, did you find peace,
In the gentle rhythm of my release?

For nine months, in your womb I grew,
A precious gift, a love so true.
In the quiet of night, did you contemplate,
The miracle of life, your heart's innate?

Mother's love, a sacred vine,
In your embrace, forever entwined.
For every kick, every tender beat,
In your love, my journey's complete.

Description:

The poem "Mother's Love, a Sacred Vine" beautifully captures the essence of the relationship between a mother and her unborn child, reflecting on the profound bond that begins even before birth. The speaker, addressing their mother, seeks to understand the emotions and experiences she must have felt while carrying them in her womb.

The poem delves into the wonder of conception and pregnancy, inviting the reader to contemplate the intricate journey of growth and development within the mother's womb. Through vivid imagery and heartfelt questions, the speaker imagines the thoughts and feelings that may have accompanied their mother during this sacred time.

The portrayal of the child's growth in the womb is depicted as a precious and miraculous process, emphasizing the awe-inspiring nature of new life. The speaker acknowledges the challenges and responsibilities faced by the mother, yet also highlights the moments of tenderness, love, and peace that undoubtedly accompanied the experience.

The title, "Mother's Love, a Sacred Vine," beautifully encapsulates the nurturing and protective nature of maternal love, likening it to a vine that binds mother and child together in an unbreakable bond. Overall, the poem celebrates the deep connection between mother and child, honouring the beauty and significance of this unique relationship from the earliest stages of life.

Poem

Dignity's Light

*In the tempest's rage, amidst the storm's plight,
My dignity stands firm, a beacon in the night.
Though others may try to tear it away,
It's a flame that burns bright, come what may.*

*When words cut deep and wounds leave scars,
My dignity remains, beneath the stars.
For it's not defined by the actions of others,
But by the strength within, like sisters and brothers.*

*They may strip me of riches, leave me in despair,
But my dignity endures, beyond compare.
It's the essence of who I am, my inner core,
A treasure untarnished, forevermore.*

*Through trials and tribulations, I'll hold it tight,
For my dignity is my guiding light.
No matter the hardships, I'll stand tall,
With dignity as my armor, I'll never fall.*

Description:

In this poem, the speaker reflects on the enduring strength of their dignity in the face of adversity. Despite being hurt and having everything taken away by people in their life, the speaker's dignity remains unshaken. The poem emphasizes the resilience of the human spirit and the intrinsic value of one's sense of self-worth.

The title, "Dignity's Light," suggests that dignity serves as a guiding force, illuminating the path forward even in the darkest times. The imagery of a beacon in the night symbolizes the unwavering nature of the speaker's dignity, offering hope and resilience.

Throughout the verses, there is a sense of empowerment and determination. The speaker acknowledges the attempts of others to diminish their dignity but asserts its enduring presence. Dignity is portrayed as a treasure, something intrinsic to the speaker's identity that cannot be taken away by external circumstances.

Overall, the poem celebrates the strength and resilience found within the human spirit, highlighting the importance of holding onto one's dignity even in the face of adversity.

Poem

Whispers in the Dark

In solitude's realm, where shadows grow long,
Loneliness whispers its melancholy song.
It wraps around hearts, a chilling embrace,
Leaving behind sorrow, in its solemn space.

Isolated souls, in the silence they dwell,
Loneliness's grip, a silent, private hell.
It paints their world in shades of blue,
Draining their spirit, till hope feels askew.

In crowded rooms, they stand alone,
Surrounded by voices, but their own they bemoan.
Their smiles may shimmer, but eyes betray,
The ache of loneliness, that won't go away.

Yet in the depths of their solitary plight,
Resides a longing for connection, so bright.
For in the warmth of companionship's embrace,
They find solace and comfort, in lover's grace.

Poem

Learning to Be Loved

In my journey through life, I thought I knew,
How to love, how to care, how to stay true.
But in the depths of my heart, I've come to see,
It's much harder to let someone love me.

From my mother's embrace, so warm and kind,
I learned to love, to cherish, to bind.
Yet in receiving love, I falter and sway,
Uncertain if I can let someone stay.

Her love was a beacon, steady and true,
Guiding me always, whatever I'd do.
But to open my heart, to let love in,
Feels like a battle I've yet to win.

For love requires vulnerability, you see,
To trust in another, to let them be.
To embrace their affection, their care, their grace,
And allow them to fill up the empty space.

So, I'll learn from my mother, wise and dear,
And bravely confront my doubts and fear.
For in learning to be loved, I'll find my way,
And bask in the warmth of love's gentle sway.

Description:

"Learning to Be Loved" delves into the complexities of accepting love from others, particularly in the context of the deep and unconditional love typically provided by a mother. The poem explores the speaker's journey of self-discovery and vulnerability, acknowledging the challenges of opening oneself up to receive love.

The title sets the stage for a reflective exploration of the speaker's emotional landscape, suggesting a process of growth and introspection. From the outset, the poem establishes a contrast between the speaker's understanding of how to love others and the difficulty they face in allowing themselves to be loved in return.

Through the imagery of a mother's love, portrayed as "bold and courageous" with a "world-beautiful soul," the poem emphasizes the nurturing and supportive role of maternal affection. However, despite being raised in an environment of love and care, the speaker grapples with the idea of reciprocating that love and accepting it from others.

The poem navigates themes of vulnerability, trust, and self-acceptance, highlighting the internal struggle faced by the speaker as they confront their own emotional barriers. There's a sense of longing and introspection as the speaker reflects on their relationship with their mother and the lessons learned from her love.

Ultimately, "Learning to Be Loved" invites readers to contemplate their own experiences with giving and receiving love, encouraging them to embrace vulnerability and trust in order to fully open their hearts to the love that surrounds them.

Poem

A Mother's Legacy

In her eyes, I found belief untold,
A mother's faith, a love so bold.
She saw in me what none could see,
And in her arms, I felt free.

Her unwavering faith became my guide,
In her love, I found my stride.
Every step I take, every dream I chase,
Is a testament to her grace.

For all I am and hope to be,
Is rooted in her legacy.
Her love has shaped me, made me whole,
A priceless gift from her soul.

So, I'll honour her with every breath,
Living up to her love until my death.
For in her belief, I find my strength,
A mother's legacy, enduring at length.

Description:

This poem, titled "A Mother's Legacy," beautifully encapsulates the profound impact of a mother's love and belief in her child. The verses speak to the deep connection between a mother and her offspring, highlighting the unwavering faith and boundless support that she offers.

The poet expresses gratitude for the mother's unwavering belief in them, acknowledging that her love has been a guiding light in their life. The imagery evokes a sense of warmth and security, as the speaker reflects on the profound influence that their mother's love has had on shaping their identity and aspirations.

Throughout the poem, there is a sense of reverence and appreciation for the sacrifices and dedication of the mother, whose love is described as bold and enduring. The speaker pledges to honour their mother's legacy by living a life that reflects the values and virtues instilled in them by her unwavering support and belief.

Overall, "A Mother's Legacy" serves as a heartfelt tribute to the transformative power of maternal love and the enduring influence that a mother's belief in her child can have on shaping their character and destiny.

Poem

Dreams With Mama

In youth, your dream, so bright it gleamed,
Of love and vows 'neath skies that teemed.
A tale you whispered, just to me,
Of love that's strong, and hearts set free.

But time slipped by, and I didn't ask,
If that dream came true or was it just a task.
Now, on life's shore, I long to see,
Your face once more, and just to be.

Memories linger, strong and true,
Your love, a beacon, shining through.
Until we meet beyond life's veil,
I'll hold your dreams, never to fail.

Description:

This poem, titled "Dreams with Mama," encapsulates the tender bond between the speaker and their mother, centered around a cherished childhood dream. The verses reflect on the dream shared by the mother, portraying it as a symbol of hope and love. The speaker recalls the dream with fondness, highlighting its significance in their relationship.

As the poem progresses, the speaker expresses regret for not inquiring about whether the dream was realized. This longing for closure underscores the theme of missed opportunities and the passage of time. Despite this, there is a sense of anticipation and yearning to reunite with the mother beyond life's confines.

The imagery evoked in the poem, such as the vibrant skies and the enduring love between mother and child, creates a poignant atmosphere. The emotions conveyed, ranging from nostalgia to hope, resonate deeply with the reader, inviting them to reflect on their own cherished memories and unfulfilled aspirations.

Overall, "Dreams with Mama" is a heartfelt exploration of love, loss, and the enduring bond between parent and child, woven together with tender rhymes and evocative imagery.

Poem

Eternal Embrace

Birthing and nurturing me, for nine months, my angelic mother,
In your embrace, I found solace like no other.
From the moment of conception, your love knew no bounds,
In your womb, I felt your heartbeat's gentle sounds.

Through the trials of pregnancy, you carried me with grace,
Each day a testament to your strength, your embrace.
With every kick and flutter, your love only grew,
In the sacred chamber of your womb, I found my debut.

Nine months of nurturing of love that knew no end,
In your arms, my journey of life began to ascend.
My angelic mother, in your love, I found my home,
Birthing and nurturing me, till eternity's dome.

In your eyes, I see a love that's pure and true.
Guiding me aways, in all that I do
Your embrace, a haven, where I find peace,
With you by my side, all worries cease

Description:

I as a child, I vividly recall the profound experience of being natured in my mother's womb for nine months and then lovingly cared for after birth. This poem serves as a deeply personal reflection on the extraordinary bond between my mother and me. It pays homage to the unwavering love, resilience, and sacrifice throughout the journey of pregnancy.

As the poet, I am deeply moved by the sheer magnitude of the love and devotion expressed by my mother. From the earliest flutter of movement in the womb to the comforting rhythm of her heartbeat, every moment shared between us is imbued with a sense of awe and reverence.

I am captivated by her unwavering commitment to my well-being, even in the face of adversity. Her grace and strength in navigating the challenges of pregnancy stand as a testament to boundless love and determination.

In crafting this poem, I am filled with a profound sense of gratitude and admiration for my mother's selflessness. It is a tribute to the enduring power of maternal love, a force that transcends boundaries and continues to inspire us for generations to come.

The final verse of the poem encapsulates the profound love and guidance provided by my mother. It underscores the purity and authenticity of her love, which serves as unwavering source of strength and reassurance. Her embrace is depicted as a sanctuary where I find solace and peace, untouched by worries or anxieties. This verse reflects my deep reverence and appreciation for my mother, highlighting the enduring bond that binds is together. Ultimately, it celebrates the timeless and unconditional nature of maternal love, with continues to nurture of maternal love, which continues to nurture and sustain me throughout my life

Poem

Mamma's Belief

*In your eyes, Mamma, I found the truth,
You saw my worth from my earliest youth.
Into my heart, you gazed so deep,
And in your faith, I found the leap.*

*You believed in me when no one else could,
Your love, Mamma, stronger than any would.
With unwavering trust, you held my hand,
Guiding me through life's shifting sand.*

*Every step I take, every path I choose,
Rooted in your belief, I'll never lose.
For what I am, and all I'll be,
Is thanks to you, Mamma, and your legacy.*

*You gave me riches beyond compare,
Not in gold or silver, but in your care.
The wealth of love you poured on me,
Is the greatest gift, for eternity.*

*So, Mamma dear, I'll make you proud,
Living up to the faith you endowed.
With every breath, I'll honour you,
For all you've done, and all you do.*

*Thank you, Mamma, for the wealth untold,
In your belief, I'll always behold.
Forever grateful, forever true,
To the one who saw my heart anew.*

Description:

This heartfelt poem titled "Mamma's Belief" beautifully expresses the deep gratitude and admiration the speaker holds for their mother. The verses reflect on the profound impact of a mother's unwavering belief in her child, even when others may doubt or misunderstand.

The poem begins with an acknowledgment of the mother's ability to see into the speaker's heart, recognizing their inherent worth and potential. This belief is portrayed as a guiding light, providing strength and encouragement throughout life's journey.

The speaker vows to honour their mother's faith by living a life that reflects the trust and confidence she had in them. They express profound appreciation for the intangible gifts of love and support bestowed upon them, acknowledging that these gifts far outweigh any material wealth.

Throughout the poem, there is a sense of deep reverence and gratitude for the mother's role in shaping the speaker's identity and guiding them towards a life filled with purpose and meaning. The sentiment expressed is one of profound love and indebtedness, as the speaker reflects on the immeasurable impact of their mother's belief in them.

Poem

Fathers Guiding Light

Father, in the quiet of my soul, I confide,
Sometimes, seeking guidance, I tend to slide.
Consulting all, except Your sacred light,
Yet, in Your wisdom, everything is set right.

I may not always embrace the answers You share,
Attempting my path, often blind to Your care.
Help me discern when I stray away,
In every decision, with You, let me stay.

Your wisdom towers, understanding profound,
Above all counsel, your grace knows no bound.
In every act, in every thought, and every endeavour,
Guide me, Father, to a life abundant, forever.

For Your love, enduring despite my defiance,
For grace that envelops, a divine alliance.
Above all, I thank You for mercy divine,
In Your embrace, my stubbornness You refine.

Poem

Eulogy:
"The Light We've Lost"

In the shadows of sorrow, we gather today,
To bid farewell as the light fades away.
A soul, guided by a wisdom divine,
A father, in memories, forever entwined.

He knew the rhythm of prayers whispered,
When we sought guidance, His light delivered.
In quiet moments, we shared our fears,
His counsel echoed in our silent tears.

A stubborn heart, His love would embrace,
Grace abundant, even in our defiance.
Mercy, a balm for wounds unseen,
In His presence, our souls serene.

The answers we sought, sometimes astray,
Yet, His love endured, guiding our way.
In every decision, His light unfurled,
A guiding force in our bewildered world.

Thank you, Father, for the love we knew,
For grace and mercy that forever grew.
In the tapestry of life, a thread now lost,
Yet, in our hearts, Your light's the cost.

Wealth Unveiled

In castles adorned with diamond and gold,
Fortunes amassed, a narrative bold.
Yet within, a truth left untold,
Innocent tears stolen, lies unfold.

Amidst the opulence, a deceptive veneer,
Broken hearts yearning, the silent fear.
Acknowledgment missing of needs untold,
For what matters when love isn't the gold?

Oh! No! When you depart this mortal stage,
Judgment awaits, the soul's righteous gauge.
Fame, Power, Wealth, they all dissolve,
Leaving echoes of deeds, a story to resolve.

Eulogy:
"A Soul's Journey Unveiled"

Gathered here, where castles fade,
A soul departed, memories cascade.
In the quest for wealth, power, and fame,
A truth obscured, an eternal flame.

Diamonds and gold, once treasures fair,
Yet, beneath the surface, the heart laid bare.
Innocent tears, tales of deception spun,
A journey of a soul, now gently done.

The earth's farewell, a judgment near,
Reflecting deeds, both far and near.
Fame, Power, Wealth, they all decay,
Leaving behind the essence of one's stay.

The mirror of the soul reveals,
The impact of fame and wealth's appeals.
Dark shadows cast on the humble path,
Yet, greatness emerges from love's aftermath.

Society may not witness the silent strife,
But the legacy left is not in gold but in life.
For in the end, it's love and empathy,
That defines the greatness of a soul set free.

Poem

Mother's Embrace

In your womb, I felt your heartbeat true,
Your love, but also pain, a tempest's brew.
Storms you faced, from your own kin,
Yet your love endured, despite the din.

I heard your weeping, felt your sorrow deep,
Helpless, I longed to soothe, to keep.
Your physical pain, fatigue so near,
Yet your heart, steadfast, devoid of fear.

For love and passion, you endured the test,
To provide a haven, a place of rest.
In your womb, I loved, I revered,
A mother's sacrifice, so clear.

From your womb, I vowed to protect,
To shield you from any pain's effect.
A mother like no other, so true,
I thank the heavens, and you.

Description:

Your description captures the essence of the profound bond between a mother and her unborn child, but there are a few areas that could be improved for clarity and flow. Here's a refined version:

"In this life-centric perspective, we delve into the profound experiences and emotions that define the relationship between my mother and me, the unborn child.

Imagine my mother, her heart brimming with love and anticipation as she carried me within her womb. From the very moment of conception, I felt a deep connection to the tiny life growing inside her. Every beat of her heart echoed in the gentle rhythm of my movements.

Yet, amidst the joy of pregnancy, my mother also grappled with her own struggles and challenges. She felt the weight of the world on her shoulders, from the stresses of daily life to the pain of past hurts and disappointments. Despite her own suffering, she found solace in the knowledge that she was nurturing new life within her.

As the months passed, my mother experienced a myriad of emotions – from the exhilaration of feeling her baby's (my) first kicks to the moments of exhaustion and uncertainty. Yet, through it all, she remained steadfast in her love and commitment to her unborn child (me).

In the quiet moments of the night, she found herself lost in contemplation, marvelling at the miracle of life growing inside her. Her whispers of love and encouragement promised to be there for me through every trial and triumph.

And when the time came for her baby to enter the world, my mother was filled with an overwhelming sense of joy and gratitude. She cradled her newborn in her arms, feeling the weight of responsibility and the boundless depth of love that only a mother can know.

In this life-centric description, we honour the sacred bond between mother and child – a bond that transcends words and defies explanation, rooted in the deepest depths of the human heart."

Poem

Eternal Love

I love you, Mother, though you're gone,
Your love, a beacon, forever drawn.
Guiding me through each step, each day,
In every aspect, lighting the way.

No other love could ever compare,
To the bond we share, so rare.
Today, tomorrow, and beyond,
In my heart, your love lives on.

Even when breath fades away,
Our love, eternal, will always stay.
For in your love, I find my light,
Guiding me through the darkest night.

Description:

In this heartfelt poem, I express the enduring love and deep connection I feel for my mother, even in her absence.

The title, "Eternal Love," sets the tone for the poem, conveying the timeless and unbreakable bond between a mother and her child. Despite my mother's physical absence, her love remains a guiding force in my life, illuminating my path and providing comfort and reassurance.

Throughout the poem, I convey the depth of my love for my mother, emphasizing that it has never wavered, even after her passing. Her love continues to be a source of strength and inspiration for me, guiding me through every aspect of my life. I am grateful for the love she bestowed upon me during her time on Earth, and I carry it with me always, like a cherished beacon of light.

I express my commitment to honouring my mother's memory by living a life filled with love, kindness, and compassion. Her love has left an indelible mark on my heart, shaping who I am today and influencing every decision I make. Even in death, our bond remains unbroken, and I find solace in the knowledge that our love is eternal.

In writing this poem, I pay tribute to the enduring love and influence of my mother, celebrating the profound impact she has had on my life and expressing gratitude for the gift of her love. It is a heartfelt declaration of the eternal connection between a mother and her child, a bond that transcends time and space.

Poem

In Every Life, I Choose You, Mother

In every life, I choose you, Mother dear,
Your love and guidance forever near.
Second only to God, your wisdom divine,
In your teachings, my devotion aligns.

Through trials and tribulations, I've faced,
Your lessons, my compass, never displaced.
Despite the brutality, the pain endured,
Your morals, steadfast, remain assured.

Each life, each incarnation, I find,
Your presence, Mother, always entwined.
For in your love, I am reborn anew,
In every life, I choose you.

Description:

In this poignant poem, I express the profound bond and enduring love between my mother and me across multiple lifetimes.

The title, "In Every Life, I Choose You, Mother," sets the tone for the heartfelt tribute that follows. It conveys the idea that regardless of the circumstances or challenges faced in each life, I would always choose my mother to be by my side.

Throughout the poem, I depict my mother as a beacon of love, wisdom, and guidance. She holds a revered place in my heart, second only to God, and her teachings serve as the cornerstone of my faith and values. Her influence on my life is profound, shaping my devotion, motivation, and inspiration in every incarnation.

Despite the trials and tribulations, I encounter, including experiences of brutality, humiliation, and physical pain, my mother's teachings remain a constant source of strength and resilience. Her moral guidance provides me with a steadfast foundation, empowering me to overcome adversity and stay true to my principles.

The imagery of choosing my mother in every life underscores the deep connection and bond that exists between us. It suggests a timeless and eternal relationship that transcends the boundaries of time and space. Across multiple lifetimes, I am drawn to her love and guidance, finding solace and renewal in her presence.

In essence, this poem is a testament to the enduring love and unwavering support of my mother. It celebrates her role as a source of comfort, inspiration, and guidance in my life, and reflects the profound impact she has had on shaping my character and values across lifetimes.

Poem

A Perfect Mother

*Mother, you were perfect in every way,
Yet, your own kin treated you astray.
Despite their doubts, you never wavered,
Your love for us, unwavering and favoured.*

*Like an ocean, vast and deep,
You carried us, though the burdens steep.
Guiding us through life's tumultuous tide,
With love and patience, you were our guide.*

*Though they saw you as a villain's name,
In our hearts, you'll forever reign.
For you, dear mother, were flawless and true,
A perfect mother in all that you do.*

Description:

In this heartfelt poem, I express my admiration and gratitude for my mother, highlighting her unwavering love and guidance despite facing challenges and adversity from those closest to her.

The title, "A Perfect Mother," sets the tone for the poem, conveying my belief in my mother's perfection and the profound impact she has had on my life. Despite any imperfections or shortcomings perceived by others, I see my mother as flawless and exemplary in her role as a mother.

Throughout the poem, I emphasize the contrast between my perception of my mother's perfection and the unjust treatment she received from her own kin. Despite being misunderstood or unfairly judged, my mother continued to love and support her children unconditionally, embodying the true essence of maternal love.

The imagery of an ocean carrying the world's load symbolizes the immense strength and resilience my mother possessed. Like the vast expanse of the ocean, she bore the weight of her responsibilities with grace and fortitude, never faltering in her commitment to her children's well-being.

Despite being cast in the role of a villain by some, my mother's love and devotion remained unwavering. In my eyes, she was and will always be a perfect mother, a beacon of love, strength, and guidance in my life.

In writing this poem, I honour the extraordinary woman who shaped me into the person I am today. It is a heartfelt tribute to my mother's selflessness, resilience, and unconditional love, celebrating her perfection in my eyes and expressing deep gratitude for her presence in my life.

Poem

Mother's Courageous Soul

*Mother, with courage bold and bright,
You faced the world with all you might.
Your soul, a beacon shining true,
Guiding us with love, through and through.*

*In storms of life, you stood so tall,
Facing challenges, big and small.
Your strength, a fortress, never swayed,
In your embrace, all fears allayed.*

*With every step, you paved the way,
For us to thrive, come what may.
Your love, a flame that brightly burned,
In every lesson, every turn.*

*Your courage, a gift we hold dear,
Inspiring us, year after year.
Mother, your soul, so beautiful and pure,
Forever in our hearts, forever sure.*

Description:

"Mother's Courageous Soul" is a heartfelt ode to a mother whose strength and bravery serve as a guiding light for her loved ones. The poem celebrates the mother's boldness and resilience in facing life's challenges, portraying her as a source of unwavering support and inspiration.

The title sets the tone for the poem, emphasizing the central theme of the mother's courageous spirit. Throughout the verses, the imagery of courage and strength is vividly depicted, painting a picture of a woman who fearlessly confronts adversity with grace and determination.

The poem acknowledges the mother's role as a beacon of hope and stability in the lives of her children and family. Her unwavering love and selflessness are highlighted as she navigates through life's trials and tribulations, always putting the well-being of her loved ones above her own.

The title, "Mother's Courageous Soul," encapsulates the essence of the poem, conveying the depth of admiration and respect for a mother whose bravery and resilience leave an indelible mark on the hearts of those around her.

Poem

A Mother's Treasure

Mother, every moment with you, a precious gem,
From childhood to now, in my heart, they stem.
The scent of your skin, the laughter we shared,
In every memory, your love declared.

Despite the burdens, you wore a smile bright,
Glowing like the sun, calming as the night.
Your strength, a force, deeper than the sea,
Wider than the world, a boundless decree.

Your wisdom, an ocean, vast and deep,
Guiding me through challenges, promises to keep.
To express my love and appreciation, I find,
No word sufficient, no phrase defined.

I loved you then, and love you more each day,
In every moment, your love lights the way.
Mother, you're a treasure, beyond compare,
In your embrace, I find solace rare.

Description:

In this heartfelt poem, we embark on a journey of appreciation, celebrating the profound bond between a mother and her child. Each verse is a testament to the enduring love and unwavering support that defines their relationship.

The poem begins with a reflection on the countless moments shared between the mother and her child since childhood. These memories are depicted as precious jewels, cherished, and treasured in the depths of the heart. The imagery of the mother's laughter, speech, singing, and dancing evokes a sense of warmth and nostalgia, transporting us back to those cherished moments of togetherness.

Despite facing challenges and hardships from others, the mother's resilience shines through. She carries herself with a radiant smile, symbolizing her inner strength and unwavering determination to overcome any obstacle. Her presence is described as comforting as the moon and as vibrant as the stars, illuminating the path forward with her love and positivity.

The mother's wisdom and strength are likened to the vastness of the ocean and the expanse of the world, emphasizing the depth and breadth of her influence in her child's life. Her guidance and support have been instrumental in shaping her child's journey, providing a steady anchor in the face of life's storms.

The poem concludes with a heartfelt declaration of love and appreciation from the child to the mother. The child expresses gratitude for the boundless love and support received from their mother, acknowledging that words alone cannot fully capture the depth of their feelings. The love shared between mother and child is depicted as a timeless and unbreakable bond, growing stronger with each passing day.

Overall, this poem serves as a beautiful tribute to the enduring love and unwavering devotion between a mother and her child, highlighting the profound impact they have on each other's lives. Through its heartfelt verses, it celebrates the beauty of maternal love and the invaluable role mothers play in shaping the lives of their children.

Poem

Mother's Grace

*In the depths of despair, in a fiery haze,
I found myself caught in a merciless craze.
A sibling's strike, a machete's cruel blow,
Left me bleeding, helpless, in the gutter's low.*

But then you came, with love in your eyes,
Your heart heavy with worry, your spirit wise.
At the hospital, fear etched upon your face,
As I lay on the table, in a precarious place.

For a year or more, you nursed me with care,
Carrying me everywhere, my burden to bear.
Your strength, a beacon in my darkest hour,
Guiding me with love, with unwavering power.

Through the pain and the tears, you never wavered,
Your love, a shelter, in which I savoured.
For your grace, your love, your endless devotion,
I am forever grateful, with deepest emotion.

Description:

In this heartfelt poem, I recount a moment of deep vulnerability and pain from my past, highlighting the unwavering support and love that my mother bestowed upon me during that challenging time.

As I reflect on the memory, I recall the harrowing ordeal of being caught in a tumultuous conflict between family members, resulting in a severe injury to my foot. The imagery of the machete's strike and the ensuing bloodshed vividly portrays the intensity and brutality of the situation, leaving me feeling helpless and alone.

However, amidst the chaos and despair, my mother emerges as a beacon of hope and comfort. Her arrival at the hospital is marked by a palpable sense of fear and concern, reflecting the depth of her love and worry for my well-being. Seeing her distress only serves to deepen my own sense of sadness and vulnerability, yet it also underscores the profound bond between us.

Over the following year, my mother becomes my unwavering caretaker and source of strength. She dedicates herself wholeheartedly to my recovery, carrying me wherever I need to go and providing the nurturing care that I require. Her resilience and determination in the face of adversity serve as an inspiration to me, giving me the strength to persevere through the pain and uncertainty.

Through her tireless efforts and boundless love, my mother becomes my rock, guiding me through the darkest moments of my life with unwavering compassion and support. Her presence is a constant source of comfort and reassurance, reminding me that I am never alone in my struggles.

Ash A. Zander
Fiery Rebirth: A Phoenix's Tale

In writing this poem, I express my deepest gratitude and appreciation to my mother for her selfless love and devotion. Her unwavering care and support have shaped me into the person I am today, and I am forever grateful for the strength and guidance she has provided me along the way.

Dance of Love

Mother, when I close my eyes,
I see you moving, graceful and wise.
Like a light feather, you float and sway,
Dancing with elegance, in your own way.

With each step, you own the floor,
Your spirit soaring, wanting more.
In your movements, love takes flight,
Filling the room with pure delight.

Your grace, a sight to behold,
Stories of love, your steps unfold.
With every twirl, every glide,
You dance with passion, by your side.

In your dance, I find solace and peace,
A moment of joy that will never cease.
Mother, your dance is a gift so rare,
A testament to the love we share.

Description:

In this heartfelt poem, I pay tribute to the beauty and grace of my mother's dance, expressing admiration and awe for her movements on the floor.

As I close my eyes, I am transported into a world where my mother's presence fills the space. I envision her moving with the lightness of a feather, her steps delicate and ethereal. Each movement is imbued with a sense of fluidity and elegance, as if she effortlessly glides across the floor.

Her dance is a sight to behold, captivating all who watch with its mesmerizing rhythm and energy. With each step, she commands the floor, her movements a reflection of her inner strength and confidence. It is as though she is in perfect harmony with the music, allowing it to guide her every movement.

As I watch her dance, I am filled with a sense of joy and admiration. Her gracefulness is truly captivating, drawing me in and leaving me in awe of her talent and beauty. In her dance, I see not only her physical prowess, but also the depth of her spirit and the love that radiates from within.

For me, her dance is more than just a series of movements—it is a testament to the love and passion that she brings to everything she does. It is a reminder of the bond we share, and the joy that she brings into my life with her presence.

In writing this poem, I seek to capture the essence of my mother's dance and the profound impact it has on me. It is a celebration of her strength, her grace, and her unwavering love—a love that shines brightly with every step she takes on the dance floor.

Poem

The Wisdom of Understanding

In wisdom's light, a truth revealed,
A wise woman's words, a sacred shield.
"For those who judge," she gently said,
"Will never grasp what lies ahead.

But those who understand, you'll find,
Hold empathy within their mind.
For judgment blinds, but empathy's grace,
Sees deeper into every face.

So let us strive to comprehend,
The hearts of others, till the end.
For in understanding's gentle touch,
We find the love that means so much.

Description:

In this poem, titled "The Wisdom of Understanding," the speaker reflects on the sage advice given to them by a wise woman. The verses delve into the profound significance of understanding versus judgment in human interactions.

The poem begins by acknowledging the wisdom imparted by the woman, emphasizing the transformative power of her words. It highlights the dichotomy between judgment and understanding, suggesting that those who judge lack the capacity to truly comprehend others, while those who understand refrain from passing judgment.

The speaker emphasizes the importance of empathy and compassion, suggesting that understanding is a pathway to deeper connection and mutual respect. By refraining from judgment and embracing understanding, individuals can foster meaningful relationships and bridge divides.

Overall, the poem celebrates the value of empathy and the transformative impact of understanding in human relationships. It serves as a reminder to approach others with an open heart and mind, seeking to understand rather than to judge.

Poem

Mother's Radiance

Mother, you were a gem, rare and divine,
A beacon of love that continues to shine.
With a heart of gold, so kind and pure,
Your love knew no bounds, of this, I am sure.

You were more than human, an angel in form,
Radiating love, through sunshine and storm.
Not only for humans, but for animals too,
Your compassion and kindness, always shone through.

You tended to nature, with tender care,
Nurturing life, everywhere.
Your touch was gentle, your spirit bright,
A guiding light, in the darkest night.

In your presence, we felt a sense of peace,
Your love and warmth never ceased.
You taught us kindness, by example true,
A legacy of love, that continues to renew.

Mother, you were one of a kind,
A rare gem, in this world of mine.
Your love and light, forever will gleam,
In our hearts, a cherished dream.

Description:

In this poem, I celebrate the remarkable qualities of my mother, portraying her as a truly exceptional individual whose kindness and compassion extend beyond the human realm.

My mother is depicted as a rare gem, possessing qualities that set her apart from others. Her heart is described as filled with love, kindness, and purity, making her a shining example of goodness in the world. Her presence is likened to that of an angel, radiating warmth and light wherever she goes.

What truly distinguishes my mother is her boundless love and care for not only humans but also animals and nature. She embodies a deep sense of empathy and compassion, extending her nurturing touch to all living beings. Whether it's tending to a wounded animal or caring for a struggling plant, she approaches every living creature with love and gentleness.

Her connection to nature is portrayed as tender and nurturing, reflecting her reverence for the natural world. She sees beauty in every living thing and is committed to protecting and preserving the environment for future generations.

Throughout the poem, my mother's presence is described as a source of comfort and peace. Her love and warmth have a transformative effect on those around her, inspiring kindness, and compassion in others. She is a guiding light in times of darkness, offering support and encouragement to all who seek her guidance.

In essence, my mother is depicted as an extraordinary individual whose love knows no bounds. Her kindness, compassion, and unwavering dedication to making the world a better place leave a lasting impression on everyone she encounters. She is truly a beacon of light and love, illuminating the lives of those fortunate enough to know her.

Building Bridges

Parents, the bridge to our past.
Their wisdom built on challenges vast.
Through trials and triumphs, they've paved the way,
Guiding us forward, day by day.

Their love, a foundation firm and strong,
An anchor in a world where we belong.
Yet sometimes, in our haste to soar,
We forget the lessons they have in store.

We may think we know it all,
Yet their experience stands tall.
Toxicity brews when pride takes hold,
And their guidance we dismiss, so bold.

But let us pause, and heed their voice,
For in their words lies a wealth of choice.
Let's build upon their sturdy base,
And cherish their wisdom, with grace.

For parents are the bridges we need,
To cross the waters, to sow the seed.
Let's honour them with love and care,
And build our futures, together we dare.

Regrets of Time Well Spent

In the dance of life, where moments flee,
We cherish time with family, with glee.
But when they depart, regrets may start,
Questions echo, tearing at the heart.

Why did I not say what I meant?
What if I had more time, I lament.
I should have cherished every embrace,
Would have made more memories, without a trace.

For those with parents, love shines bright,
In their presence, days feel light.
But when they leave, regrets may bloom,
In the silence, echoes of their room.

Yet in the end, we must find solace,
In the memories, where love's embrace bolsters.
For though regrets may cloud our sight,
Their love remains, a guiding light.

Description:

This poem, titled "Regrets of Time Well Spent," delves into the bittersweet emotions that accompany the passing of loved ones, particularly parents. It highlights the poignant reality that even when we have cherished moments with our parents, their departure can still leave us grappling with regrets and what-ifs.

The verses capture the universal experience of reflecting on missed opportunities and wishing for more time with those we hold dear. The regrets expressed in the poem—"Why did I not say what I meant?", "What if I had more time, I lament", "I should have cherished every embrace", "Would have made more memories, without a trace"— underscore the profound impact that the loss of a parent can have on one's sense of closure and fulfillment.

Despite the sadness and remorse that may accompany the passing of parents, the poem also emphasizes the importance of finding solace in the cherished memories and love shared with them. The final lines convey a message of hope and resilience, reminding us that even in the face of regrets, the enduring presence of a parent's love can serve as a guiding light through life's journey.

Poem

Unspoken Strength

How did you do it, dear mother mine,
Enduring ridicule, yet with grace you shine?
Day in and out, your own children's jest,
Yet in the eyes of the world, you're truly blessed.

Your secret strength, you held it tight,
Beneath your smile, hid a silent fight.
Valued and loved by the community's gaze,
Your inner turmoil concealed in a silent maze.

What was your secret, mother dear?
That shielded you from every tear.
You took it with you to the grave's silent rest,
Leaving your children to ponder, to jest.

Your unspoken strength, a beacon bright,
Guiding us through the darkest night.
Though your secret remains a mystery untold,
Your legacy of resilience and love, forever bold.

Description:

This poem delves into the profound strength and resilience exhibited by a mother who faces ridicule from her own children while still being cherished and respected by the wider community. The speaker, likely one of the children, reflects on their mother's ability to endure such emotional pain while maintaining her composure and dignity.

The poem explores the contrast between the mother's public image of strength and the internal struggles she faces. Despite the challenges she endures within her own family, she remains a pillar of strength and love in the eyes of the community.

The speaker expresses a sense of awe and admiration for their mother's ability to keep her emotions hidden, pondering the secret behind her unwavering resolve. The mother's resilience becomes a source of inspiration, symbolizing the quiet strength that lies within her.

Ultimately, the poem reflects on the complexity of human emotions and the depth of a mother's love, even in the face of adversity. It highlights the unspoken sacrifices and challenges that mothers often face, offering a poignant tribute to their enduring strength and love.

Poem

A Brother Heartbeat

*In the pure symphony of brotherly love,
Through thick and thin, below, and above.
A language understood by Mom and the Divine,
You, my pillar, in every trial, in every line.*

*Shouldering pain, a mirror of Mom care,
Beside me, vowed as Mom whispers filled the air.
In sorrow shadow, with our drainage sibling near,
Protector then, protector now, sincere.*

*You wear our mother heart, so kind,
Names echo, a shared legacy bind.
Brother, a guide through life vast sea,
Enlightenment found in love decree.*

*Comparisons fade with a drainage sibling quest,
Unique paths, each with its own test.
Keep your eyes open, do good, pour love,
Define your worth, rise above."*

Description

A Brother Heartbeat resonates with the profound bond between siblings, particularly, celebrating the love and support given by the brother. The poem recognizes the unique language of understanding shared by family members, specifically between the poet and their brother, acknowledged by Mom and the Creator.

The verses delve into the brother role as a protector, mirroring the care bestowed by their mother. It addresses shared vows made in the face of adversity and acknowledges the pain. endured alongside a drainage sibling. The poem encourages the brother not to compare his journey but to find enlightenment in pouring love into his own life and family.

The dedication to Virend Kumaran expresses deep appreciation for his role as a brother, emphasizing his kindness, guidance, and unique journey. It encourages him to define his worth, rise above challenges, and highlights the enduring support from sister Ashley.

The description underscores the human-centric theme of familial bonds, love, and the individual
intrinsic value.

Dedication To Virend Kumaran

In the tapestry of life, your role as a brother shines bright. Your unwavering love and protective spirit echoes the kindness found in our dear mother heart. Your journey, unique and valuable, deserves to be celebrated. Keep your eyes open and let the love you poured into the lives of those around you be a testament to your goodness. Sis Ashley stands by your side, a testament to the enduring bond of family. You are a god-sent angel, and this poem is. A tribute to the remarkable person you are.

Poem

Bonds Beyond Blood

In the realm of care, a journey unfolds,
With an autistic heart, a story retold.
A mingling of emotions, both joy and scorn,
For the growth observed, a transformative morn.

Biological ties may not bind our space,
Yet, in my heart, you find a cherished place.
Flash and bones, a metaphorical embrace,
A connection profound, defying time, and space.

Imagination falls short to describe,
The bond that blossoms as we both thrive.
Each day a canvas, our shared bong,
A blessing from above, where we both belong.

As a growing child, you teach and inspire,
Through moments shared, our souls conspire.
Closer we grow, in a human centred theme,
A testament to love, beyond the extreme.

To the parents, gratitude I send,
For entrusting me, a bond to tend.
The trust bestowed, a gift so rare,
In this shared journey, we a trio rare.

Description

Bonds Beyond Blood is a heartwarming and reflective poem that explores the unique and profound connection between a caregiver and an autistic child. The title encapsulates the essence of the verses, emphasizing the theme of familial bonds that transcend biological ties.

The poem navigates the nuanced emotions of joy and, surprisingly, scorn that come with witnessing the growth of an autistic client. It speaks to the depth of the connection, comparing it to a familial bond, with the metaphor of flash and bones conveying a sense of shared identity.

The verses celebrate the everyday moments shared, describing them as a blessing from above. The term symbolizes the shared experiences and the intimate connection formed through time spent together. The gratitude expressed to the parents acknowledges the trust placed in the caregiver, creating a rare and cherished trio in this Life's-centric narrative.

Overall, the poem is a testament to the power of love, connection, and the transformative nature of caregiving relationships that go beyond traditional family structures.

Poem

Love Intrinsic Thread

"In the tapestry of existence, a thread profound,
Love, a whisper in every heartbeat, all around.
Part of life fabric, woven intricately,
A constant presence, an eternal decree.

It the gentle breeze in the morning air,
The warmth that weaves through moments rare.
Love in a smile, a tender embrace,
A silent language, a universal grace.

In the human heart, its residence found,
A symphony of emotions, forever bound.
It the laughter shared in joyous mirth,
A dance in tune with life rhythmic birth.

Love is the compass in the darkest night,
A beacon that guides, a soothing light.
Part of life journey, a steadfast guide,
In every ebb and flow, by our side.

Description:

At its core, the poem conveys the idea that love is a ubiquitous force that shapes our experiences and perspectives. The title, Intrinsic Thread, suggests that love is not an isolated element but an essential and interconnected part of the intricate fabric of life.

The verses describe love as a pervasive force, manifesting in various forms, from the gentle breeze to the shared laughter and residing deeply within the human heart. The poem encapsulates the idea that love is an enduring companion, offering comfort, joy, and guidance throughout the journey of life.

Poem

Treasured Moments with My Boy

After a long wait, 12/23, a blessed day unfolds,
11.30 on the clock, joy in the hours it holds.
Drove up, picked him up, a lunchtime quest,
Together we laughed, in shared moments, blessed.

Mario world, our playful delight,
Video games dancing in laughter light.
Old memories revisited, a nostalgic flight,
My boy and I, in love sweetest height.

His hands around my neck, a cherished link,
The world most expensive jewel, distinct.
No wealth compares, no matter how succinct,
A rare gem, in love treasury succinct.

He holds my heart, a world so grand,
A wealth beyond measure, like grains of sand.
No money in this world can understand,
The depth of love, like an ocean so grand.

Beyond imagination, my love takes flight,
A bond unbreakable, a sacred rite.
This boy of mine, my eternal light,
In the tapestry of love, endlessly bright.

Dedication to my boy *Filipp Urovsiky*

In every moment shared, in every laugh and play,
You are the treasure that brightens my day.
Your hands around my neck, a jewel so divine,

No amount of wealth can match the love you shine.
You are my biggest wealth, my rarest find,
A gym of love, one of its kind.
Beyond all riches, beyond gold sheen,
In your love, my heart is forever serene.

Description:

The poem unfolds as a narration of a blessed day spent with the boy, starting with the anticipation at 16:23 and driving up for a lunchtime adventure. The shared moments, playing Mario video games, and revisiting old memories evoke joy and laughter.

The boy becomes the focal point, described as the holder of the poet heart and the world most expensive jewel. The dedication emphasizes the unique bond shared, highlighting the boy significance as the poet biggest wealth and a rare gem.

The poem description explores the depth of love and the immeasurable value of these moments. The dedication is a heartfelt expression of the poet love and gratitude, acknowledging the boy as a treasure beyond any material wealth. The concluding lines emphasize the enduring brightness of this love in the tapestry of their shared journey.

Poem

Harmony Restored:
A Journey of Love and Acceptance

"In November embrace, a tale took its start,
You entered her life, mending each heart.
Amid pain and strife, a love did bloom,
A union destined, escaping the gloom.

Facing storms together, hand in hand,
Your love endured, a bond firmly planned.
Strengths and weaknesses, a blend so sweet,
Compromises made, love dance complete.

No room for kids, in the beginning phase,
The focus was building, amidst love maze.
Seven years passed, a journey well-trod,
Acceptance blossomed, a love sent from God.

In 2022, the children arrived,
A new chapter opened, and you thrived.
Father figure you became, strong and true,
A love story evolving, not just for two.

I apologize for doubts that clouded my view,
Torn between worlds, my heart misconstrued.
You shone through, a beacon so bright,
Mending the family dynamic, bringing joy and light.

Now laughter resounds, love fills each day,
Life sanctuary found in your gentle sway.
To my beautiful boys, you a guide and a friend,
Harmony restored, love journey won end."

Description:

This rhyming ode captures a journey of love and acceptance that unfolded in November 2015. Starting with pain and misery, the relationship blossomed into a resilient bond, weathering storms hand in hand. The dance of strengths and weaknesses, compromises, and a focus on building laid the foundation. Seven years later, full acceptance of the children bloomed in 2022, marking a transformative shift.

The apology in the poem acknowledges the challenges of accepting change. The arrival of the children marked a new chapter, with you evolving into a father figure. The poem celebrates your role in mending the family dynamic, bringing joy and light to everyone involved. The final stanzas express gratitude for the laughter and love that now fill each day, turning life into a sanctuary for the boys and symbolizing the restoration of harmony in the family.

Dedication To *Faizal Hamdan*

In honour of Faizal Hamdan, the steadfast architect of love journey, whose presence and dedication shaped the verses of this poem. From the initial embrace in 2015 to the transformative year of 2022, your commitment to mending the family dynamic is woven into the very fabric of our lives.

Faizal, you emerged as more than a partner but as a beacon of strength, navigating the storms and building bridges of understanding. Your resilience and love became the guiding force that led to the full acceptance of our blended family.

This dedication extends deep gratitude for your unwavering spirit, for becoming a father figure to my boys, and for transforming our lives into a sanctuary of joy and laughter. The verses penned here are a testament to your pivotal role in restoring harmony, making our shared journey a symphony of love and acceptance.

Poem

Dreams of Us- from 32992

In the realm of dreams, a tale unfolds,
Of you and me, a story never told.
At the airport, our first embrace,
Excitement and shyness on each face.

A sweet hug shared, a kiss on the chin,
Your joy, my happiness begin.
Tears in your eyes, a fear untold,
I comfort you, a promise to hold.

In the car, on the journey home,
Anticipation, no need to roam.
Excitement bubbling, smiles persist,
A homecoming, the joy we resist.

Upstairs, in the quiet room,
Emotions bloom, dispelling gloom.
Laughter, talks, and shared delight,
An evening bathed in love soft light.

Clothes shed, a dance of intimacy,
A warm shower, a shared decree.
The bedroom adorned, wine in hand,
Our hearts entwined, a love so grand.

Smiles linger, happiness prevails,
Kisses shared, a love that sails.
A dream woven, in passion embrace,
A memory etched, time cannot erase.

Description:

Dreams of Us invites readers into a dreamlike narrative, recounting an intimate and joyful encounter between two individuals. The title encapsulates the essence of the poem, emphasizing the dreamlike quality of the depicted scenario.

The poem takes the reader through a journey of excitement, tenderness, and shared happiness. The detailed description Of the dream includes moments of emotional connection, comfort, and intimacy, creating a vivid and heartfelt portrayal. The overarching theme is the celebration of love and connection in a dream world where joy and happiness intertwine.

Poem

A Prayer for the End of the Workday

As the day draws to a close, our toil we suspend,
In this moment of quiet, our weary hearts on on mend.

Grant us peace, O gracious guide,
As we leave our tasks and worries aside.

For the labor we've given, for the efforts we've shown,
For the challenges met and the seeds we've sown,

May our work be fruitful, may it bring us delight,
And may we find solace in the coming night.

Bless our colleagues, our friends, and our kin,
With joy in their hearts and a hope deep within.

As we bid farewell to the duties of day,
Grant us rest, O Lord, as we kneel down to pray.

In the twilight's embrace, let us find release,
And may tomorrow bring blessings, joy, and peace.

Description:

In this rhyming poem, the focus is on the human experience at the close of a day's work. The title sets the tone by indicating that it is a prayer, suggesting a sense of reverence and solemnity. The poem acknowledges the fatigue and challenges that come with work, but also emphasizes the importance of finding peace and solace as the day comes to an end.

Throughout the poem, there is a sense of gratitude for the labor that has been done and a hope for its fruits to be realized. The imagery evokes a feeling of winding down, of letting go of the day's burdens and worries. There's also an emphasis on community and connection, as the prayer extends blessings to colleagues, friends, and loved ones.

Overall, the poem serves as a heartfelt invocation for rest, rejuvenation, and the promise of a new day ahead.

www.ingramcontent.com/pod-product-compliance
Lightning Source LLC
Chambersburg PA
CBHW050729010526
44107CB00009B/791